FAULKNER'S CAREER

FAULKNER'S CAREER

An Internal Literary History

GARY LEE STONUM

Cornell University Press

ITHACA AND LONDON

International Standard Book Number 0-8014-1196-3
Library of Congress Catalog Card Number 78-23503
Printed in the United States of America
*Librarians: Library of Congress cataloging information appears on the last page of
the book.*

Contents

	Preface	7
	Abbreviations	9
1	*Career as Discipline*	13
2	*Visionary Poetics*	41
3	*The Search for a Narrative Method*	61
4	*The Referential Phase*	94
5	*The Fate of Design*	123
6	*Elegy as Meta-Fiction*	153
7	*The Character of the Author*	195
	Index	203

Preface

This book investigates the course of Faulkner's literary career; in particular, it is concerned to account for changes in style, theme, method, and aesthetic principle that define each phase of that career. My guiding question, in effect, is how does Faulkner know what to write next? What conditions the possibilities that are open to him at any given moment? I believe that such questions point a new direction in Faulkner criticism and also that along the way they suggest a method of exploring the careers of a good many other writers.

If the book fulfills these aims at all, its success owes a great deal to the help I have received from numerous people and from several institutions. My research began several years ago under the guidance of Laurence B. Holland and J. Hillis Miller. Most of the writing was done during the year I spent at the School of Criticism and Theory of the University of California at Irvine. There I benefited greatly from the advice and criticism of the other resident fellows: Ralph Freedman, Gary Shapiro, Gabrielle Verdier, Patricia Tobin, and Joel Weinsheimer. Paul Miers, Roger B. Salomon, John Carlos Rowe, and Frank Lentricchia have also read and commented on portions of the manuscript.

I am grateful to the National Endowment for the Humanities for a grant under the Summer Stipend program, which enabled me to complete the research, and to the School of Criticism and Theory for the fellowship that allowed me to finish the writing.

Three libraries gave me access to collections of Faulkner's manuscripts and permission to quote from unpublished poems in their possession: the Humanities Research Center, The University of Texas at Austin; the William Faulkner Collections at the University of Virginia Library; and the Henry W. and Albert A. Berg Collection, The New York Public Library, Astor, Lenox, and Tilden Foundations. In each case I was assisted by an able and friendly staff.

For permission to quote from Faulkner's copyrighted works, including his unpublished poetry, I am grateful to Mrs. Jill Faulkner Summers. Lines from *The Marble Faun* (Copyright, 1924, by The Four Seas Company, and Renewed 1952, by William Faulkner) and *A Green Bough* (Copyright, 1933, and Renewed 1960, by William Faulkner) appear with the permission of Random House, Inc.

A portion of Chapter 4 appeared in *Renascence* (Winter 1976); I thank that journal for permission to use the copyrighted material.

I would also like to thank my indexer, Kathleen L. Kemp.

GARY LEE STONUM

Cleveland, Ohio

Abbreviations

Faulkner's works, including volumes of interviews, letters, and classroom talks, will be cited parenthetically in the text and identified by the following abbreviations.

AA   *Absalom, Absalom!* (New York: Modern Library, 1951), first edition 1936.

AILD   *As I Lay Dying* (New York: Modern Library, 1967), collated from the 1930 first edition and author's manuscript by James B. Meriwether.

CS   *Collected Stories of William Faulkner* (New York: Random House, 1950).

EPP   *William Faulkner: Early Prose and Poetry,* Carvel Collins, ed. (Boston: Little, Brown, 1962).

ESPL   *Essays, Speeches, and Public Letters of William Faulkner,* James B. Meriwether, ed. (New York: Random House, 1966).

FU   *Faulkner in the University: Class Conferences at the University of Virginia, 1957–58,* Frederick L. Gwynn and Joseph L. Blotner, eds. (New York: Vintage, 1965).

GB   *A Green Bough,* photographic reproduction of the 1933 first edition; included in the volume *The Marble Faun & A Green Bough* (New York: Random House, 1965).

GDM   *Go Down, Moses* (New York: Modern Library, 1955), first edition, entitled *Go Down, Moses and Other Stories,* 1942.

H   *The Hamlet* (New York: Random House, 1940).

LA   *Light in August* (New York: Modern Library, n.d.), photographic reproduction of the 1932 first edition.

LG   *Lion in the Garden: Interviews with William Faulkner, 1926–62,*

	Michael Millgate and James B. Meriwether, eds. (New York: Random House, 1968).
M	*The Mansion* (New York: Random House, 1959).
MF	*The Marble Faun*, photographic reproduction of the 1924 first edition; included in the volume *The Marble Faun & A Green Bough* (New York: Random House, 1965).
Mq	*Mosquitoes* (New York: Liveright, 1955), first edition 1927.
NOS	*William Faulkner: New Orleans Sketches*, Carvel Collins, ed. (New York: Random House, 1958).
P	*Pylon* (New York: Modern Library, 1967), photographic reproduction of the 1935 first edition.
S	*Sanctuary* (New York: Modern Library, 1932), first edition 1931.
SF	*The Sound and the Fury* (New York: Modern Library, 1966), photographic reproduction of the 1929 first edition with the 1946 "Compson Appendix" added.
SL	*Selected Letters of William Faulkner*, Joseph Blotner, ed. (New York: Random House, 1977).
SP	*Soldiers' Pay* (New York: Liveright, 1970), first edition 1926.
T	*The Town* (New York: Random House, 1957).
WP	*The Wild Palms* (New York: Random House, 1939).

FAULKNER'S CAREER

1

Career as Discipline

No one doubts that Faulkner had a literary career, but hardly anyone has considered the fact to be of much interest. Certainly, Faulkner criticism has found no need to resort to the concept of the career in answering the questions it has addressed. Yet the broadest of these questions seem to bear closely on the shape of Faulkner's career and the path of its development. What, for example, does the supposedly grim and majestic novelist of the 1930s have to do with the embarrassingly Polonius-like figure of the 1950s, who made such floridly cheerful pronouncements in person and in print? How is it that the novelist came to write so well and so distinctively in the 1930s after a decade spent creating second-rate pastiches of decadent verse? What is the relation between Faulkner's avowal of the most traditional humanistic values—especially in the 1950s but earlier as well—and his startling innovations in literary technique? And, most notoriously of all, what is to be made of his perverse insistence that each and every one of his books, especially the best of them, is a failure?

In the following pages I mean to offer some answers to these questions and also to demonstrate more fully that all of them spring from a single, more fundamental problem faced by the writer: how to establish and maintain a career. The guiding purpose is neither to offer readings of Faulkner's books nor to elucidate the general themes present throughout his work, although I will also be doing both these things. My intention is to show that Faulkner's care for his career gives his writings a systematic regularity. The investigation will accordingly differ from the kind of enterprise that had dominated Faulkner criticism for many years. Although this regularity is related to the formal and thematic patterns of individual texts and to the thematic continuities in his work as a whole, it is not wholly congruous with either of these familiar objects of critical discourse.

To a considerably greater degree than has been recognized, Faulkner's writings belong to a career that is itself an important factor in the production of new work. The career, the ongoing course of writing, has its own distinctive properties and its own independent coherence. The coherence is no simple unity; it cannot be grasped as a tidy linear unfolding, for example, or a process of steady, organic growth. Faulkner's development is not to be explained by a single, encompassing term for the cohesiveness of all his writings nor even by a set of terms that would establish the precise boundaries of his literary universe. Instead, it is a cumulative process of change in which temporary unities are continually dissolved and then reorganized as new work is produced. The process is not random, but nor is it governed by a single program of transformations. It works rather by an internal and, as it were, self-governing regularity.

Before this regularity can be explored in any detail, it is necessary to ask what in general a literary career might be. Does the term actually name some phenomenon that may become a specific object of study? My discussion pertains chiefly to Faulkner, of course, but if the approach possesses any cogency it should not be limited to him. Hence in defining the notion of career and in explaining how Faulkner's can be investigated, I shall take some care to situate the relevant issues within a broad spectrum of critical theories and methods.

Modern criticism employs the word "career" regularly and innocuously, but only rarely asks what is meant in saying that writers have such things.[1] In fact, the term does not usually designate a concept that is especially troublesome or even noticeably distinct from the writer's life (as recounted in biography), from his works (as expounded in commentary), or from both of them together (as portrayed in critical biography). For example, the only other book on Faulkner that has the word in its title is a bibliography: to the author of that book, James Meriwether, Faulkner's literary career is identical with his literary output, and rightly so considering the normal uses of the term.[2] It is possible, however, to identify a third sense of career, which lies midway between life and works, and to argue that such a concept can offer a distinctive way of understanding how literary texts come into existence.

The most important application of the third usage to Faulkner's work is the idea of career as the relation between the results of a course of writing and the furtherance of that course, that is, between the texts a writer has already written and the writing of new texts. A career thus has two familiar aspects which are roughly analogous to life and works in that one refers to an ongoing activity and the other to a completed body of work. The one is the projected career that a writer intends to continue as he produces new work, whereas the other is the past career he has already achieved in his previous output. In Faulkner's case—and in the case of many other writers who embark upon a serious

1. A notable exception and an important influence on my own work is Edward Said in *Beginnings: Intention and Method* (New York 1975), especially 227–275.

2. James B. Meriwether, *The Literary Career of William Faulkner* (Princeton 1961), reprinted in 1971 by the University of South Carolina Press.

literary project, I would argue—the significant phenomenon is the relation between these two aspects. Career as past output becomes an active force in shaping career as continued production. For the writer to pursue such a career is for him to fasten his writing to the possibility of orderly progress that we commonly refer to as "development." The career becomes a kind of discipline to which the writer submits himself.

A career is by definition something that occurs one step at a time. It happens or is made first of all by a preliminary intention to make it happen, an intention which may well precede any sure understanding of what the career is to be. This seems to be the case with Faulkner; he set out first of all to be a writer and only then began discovering what kind of writer he could be. In later years he recalled that he had already fully comitted himself to a literary vocation by 1923; by that date it was already a "fate" with its own demands upon him. "I wrote a book and discovered that my doom, fate, was to keep on writing books: not for any exterior or ulterior purpose: just writing the books for the sake of writing the books" (*ESPL* 180). His biographer supposes that Faulkner's earliest surviving poems date from around 1916, when Faulkner was about nineteen.[3] One may go back much further still, for Faulkner is said to have told his third-grade classmates on several occasions that "I want to be a writer."[4] The date is unimportant; what matters is that Faulkner's intention preceded by many years the writing of the works that are most interesting to us today. Implementing this intention gave rise to a long series of transforma-

3. Joseph Blotner, *Faulkner: A Biography* (New York 1974), I, 184–186.
4. The story may be apocryphal. It was first reported by Robert Coughlan in *The Private World of William Faulkner* (New York 1954), 33–34. Blotner's biography repeats the story but cites only Coughlan as a source.

tions, reappraisals, and altered understandings of what being a writer entailed. These changes comprise much of the particular coherence of Faulkner's career. They form a procession that begins with the relatively empty and vague intention to be a writer, finds its first concrete manifestation in the production of one kind of text, and then changes and keeps on changing as a result of what the already produced texts open up or point him toward. Each new text is, of course, a singular and precarious venture whose outcome is affected by all sorts of contingencies. But it is also part of a systematic process which alters the intention to be a writer as it helps to fulfill it.[5]

It is commonly recognized that a literary career can have its own direction and momentum. Book reviewers frequently and accurately speak of some new text as continuing the previous course of a writer's work or, alternately, as breaking new ground for him and opening up new territory that he can explore further. The reviewer reading a new book necessarily catches the writer's career in its most fundamental mode, as the middle of something not yet complete. For a writer to be engaged in a career is necessarily for him always to be in mid-course, regarding and perhaps responding to the now fixed past which is his output to date and anticipating an uncertain future in which he intends to continue writing. Like each new text, the career is something the writer produces. But because he always continues to be producing it until he stops writing entirely, it can also

5. In discussing this process I will use throughout the order in which the books were published. In some cases, notably *A Fable,* the writing extended over many years and was interrupted by the writing and publication of other books. But the novels on which Faulkner worked the longest were, of course, those he revised and rewrote the most. Their form is determined by his final decisions and not his early intentions. For more arbitrary reasons, mainly those of keeping this study of manageable scope, I will generally neglect the place of the short stories in Faulkner's career.

be something in which he is caught up or to which he belongs while producing texts. The more this is so, the more the career will develop as a system with its own rules and regularities and the more it will reflect the exigencies of the discipline to which the writer has submitted himself.

Adherence to discipline blurs the categories of subjectivity and personal autonomy that most of us often unthinkingly apply to an individual's actions. Discipline can mean both an external regimen, which an individual adopts, and an internal self-discipline, which is one of the chief determinants of individuality as such. The distinction is more logical than practical, for who can really distinguish the determined individuality of a great musician, say, from the regimen in which his talent is both manifested and developed? To a considerable degree, the musician *qua* musician is the result of his hours of study, practice, and performance, but he is also, of course, the subject who works to cause the result. Syntactically speaking, reflexive verbs would supply the most appropriate predicates for such a produced/producing individual, and so also for a literary career. A career can be both a product that the writer creates and an agency that helps to create him as a writer. The reciprocity between the subjectivity of the creator and the objectivity of the creation is actually a common enough phenomenon, but its operation has been to some extent obscured by the widespread idea of the artist as a free and autonomous subject whose work springs primarily from the internal depths of genius or native talent.

It will be useful in the following pages to distinguish the two subjectivities implicated in a writing career. I will reserve the term "author" exclusively for the subject produced by the writing and "writer" primarily for the subject who produces it. (Both are, of course, abstractions from the historical personage William Faulkner.) To write is to perform the function that will be our primary concern. To be an author is to have performed this function in such a way that one's writings are viewed as a distinct, coherent corpus.

The author (like *l'auteur* as distinguishable from *l'ecrivain* or *der Dichter* from *der Schriftsteller*) is the more majestic figure. We impute to him the unity, meaning, and truth of his work. Authorship in this respect is a badge of authority, as the common root of the two words suggests. Authoritative writings such as great poems, historically significant documents, and important scientific treatises have authors; interoffice memoranda and pulp fiction usually have only writers. A coherent career is, of course, no guarantee of authority or of stature as an author. But one kind of authority is that which accrues from a recognition that individual texts lie within a larger project with its own import and coherence. If Max Brod had destroyed Kafka's manuscripts as he was ordered, the few pieces Kafka had published would have hardly constituted such a meaningful ensemble. The authority we would be able to discern in the published texts alone would surely be less than what we recognize in them as parts of Kafka's full career and as stages in his austere development. For one's texts to belong to a career can thus give them an authority they would not possess singly. For the writer to pursue such a career is for him to be responsible for the ongoing coherence of his writing and responsive to it. Such responsibility and responsiveness would then characterize the adherence to a discipline that he both creates and is created by in becoming an author.

The coherence possible in a career differs from the sorts of order which are studied in two other important kinds of critical enterprise. A comparison will help us see what is at stake in examining Faulkner's career. On one side is exegetical criticism, which pursues a coherence of form and meaning at the level of the individual text. Most American criticism of Faulkner has been of this sort; it is usually allied at least loosely with New Critical close reading.[6] A very similar kind of criticism seeks to talk not only about individual texts but the author's work as a whole. It accordingly faces a somewhat different problem and often seeks coherence also at the level of the author's vision of truth.[7] Opposite exegetical criticism stand the several kinds of criticism that make up theoretical poetics. These pursue structural coherences at the level of some transindividual unit such as genre, tradition, or literature in general. Those which are not simply taxonomies are often particularly interested in the limits or restraints on literature and in what a particular literary structure allows or excludes. Probably the most influential representative of this sort of criticism in the English-speaking world is Northrop Frye; most structuralist and poststructuralist European criticism is also of this sort.[8]

These various kinds of regularity are by no means incompatible with one another, but a critical enterprise that takes one or another as its goal often makes a very distinctive claim about the writer's freedom of expression and about the resulting relation between an author and his works. Exegetical criticism tends to emphasize the singularity of the text and hence the originality and freedom of the writer who has created it. Meaning in a text is generally ascribed to the writer's spontaneous creativity or at least to his free choice among forms of expression. This is especially so now that the New Critical dread of the intentional fallacy, never all that strong among critics of fiction anyway, has largely

6. The most distinguished book-length example of this sort of criticism is Olga Vickery's *The Novels of William Faulkner* (Baton Rouge, La. 1964), rev. ed.

7. For example, Cleanth Brooks's *William Faulkner: The Yoknapatawpha Country* (New Haven 1966).

8. Frye's *Anatomy of Criticism* (Princeton 1957) differs markedly from more recent theory of this kind in that he doesn't suppose existing literary structures to burden the writer.

dissipated.[9] Theoretical poetics, in contrast, tends to dissolve the specificity of individual texts and to see them as taking a place in an already constituted structure of discourse. The writer thus is considerably less free and at the extreme is even limited to performing functions already specified in a larger structure. In exegetical criticism the text is the writer's own; in poetics it often belongs to the structure.

The relevance to Faulkner's work of this dispute about freedom and possession can be confirmed by noticing that it is directly analogous to the debate between Ike McCaslin and McCaslin Edmonds in *Go Down, Moses.* Both characters recognize the powerful system of exploitation and injustice that Carothers McCaslin had inaugurated on the plantation with such awesome authority. Ike, who argues that the fraudulent possession of the land is man's primordial crime, sees that men are themselves possessed by the illusion of ownership to perpetuate a system that enslaves them all, black and white. But he believes that the individual has autonomy enough at least to relinquish his inheritance of a place within the system, to choose the alternate paternity of the wilderness, and thus to be free. His cousin, in response, resolutely denies that an individual can make himself free by repudiating the system that has engendered him. "I am what I am; I will be always what I was born and have always been. And more than me" (*GDM* 300). What concerns us here is not the familiar pertinence of their debate to Faulkner's heritage as a Southerner but the implications for Faulkner's heritage as a writer and for his place within the literary traditions that have helped to engender his writing.

The question is the kind and the degree of constraint on a

9. Most Faulkner commentary posits a role for the author essentially similar to the one advocated by the title and text of Mark Spilka's "The Necessary Stylist," reprinted in *Issues in Contemporary Literary Criticism,* Gregory Polletta, ed. (Boston 1973), 207–214.

writer demanded by the larger systems of literary discourse. It is generally agreed that literature is not produced with the freedom by which God created the world or even that by which Adam, the first poet, named its inhabitants. Rather, the writer must accede to a discipline, however defined and however rigorous or systematic, which in return for teaching him what literature is and what the possibilities within it might be for him, necessarily limits his freedom of expression. The discipline of literature is thus both a constraint on a writer and what makes it possible for him to write at all. He learns to write, among other ways, by reading what others have written, and he perhaps learns also in the process something more concrete about what one may hope to achieve by writing. The lazy or unsophisticated writer may learn only enough to repeat unawares the received formulas of his culture. The ambitious and skillful writer, we like to think, understands his situation better and writes with enough awareness and determination so as not to remain wholly the unwitting slave of the already written.

Modern poetics has increasingly emphasized the power of this general discipline, to which every writer must submit.[10] Its challenge to the claims of the individual writer's sovereignty usually takes the form of an exploration of some particular constraint upon literary production. Frequently enough, the constraint proves to be not simply a limitation

10. A striking indication of this tendency is supplied by David Carroll's essay about Hayden White's *Metahistory*, "On Tropology: The Forms of History," *Diacritics*, 6 (Fall 1976), 58–64. White's book (Baltimore 1974) is itself an important work in the tradition of modern poetics. It argues that the strategies of nineteenth-century historians and philosophers of history were prefigured and constrained by the four principal rhetorical tropes: metaphor, metonymy, synecdoche, and irony. Carroll contends that White does not go far enough in his analysis and that he continues to defend the autonomous subject's free choice among tropes which otherwise determine the historical discourse.

but an active source of exigency. Ignoring the considerable differences that exist among such critics and theorists, we can isolate three constraints commonly argued to limit the possibilities of literature. These are the restrictions imposed by the nature of language, by the preexisting literary tradition, and by the writer's social and historical environment. Each of these contributes to establishing boundaries upon what is possible for a writer, and each presents a challenge that the writer is obliged to face.[11]

These constraints represent three aspects of the general discipline in which a writer works and three structures in which his writing is confined. To these we may add a fourth, unequal, partner—the writer's relationship to his own career, or more specifically to his own past writings and to the possibility of continuing to write. It is an unequal partner because it is capable of subserving the other three and yet remains less universal than any of them. No solemn law of literature requires a writer to take account of his own previous writings or to conceive of his career as anything more demanding than a means of paying his bills and occupying time. Many writers, Faulkner included, take such account, but this is by no means as obligatory as taking account of language. On the other hand, to the extent that a writer's career attains a kind of coherence or aspires to it, the career will be the stage on which his response to the other three constraints is chiefly played out. The transformations in his career will show forth his relationships to his literary predecessors, for example, much more fully than any single text he writes.

Without further specification the three constraints I have ascribed to poetics are too blunt to be useful instruments for

11. To document the recent interest in such general constraints would require a chapter-length digression. In lieu of that, let me name here only those theorists who seem to me the most important and influential: Jacques Derrida, Harold Bloom, and Michel Foucault.

analyzing Faulkner's career. We can, however, point the way to a closer analysis and also examine the relationship between the discipline of a career and the discipline of literature in general by considering Geoffrey Hartman's thesis about how tradition and environment operate together.[12] Hartman suggests that we think of the writer's individual genius as necessarily subject to two relationships, one with "Genius"—that is, with the literary tradition and with the forms and achievements of earlier writers—and the other with "*genius loci*"—that is, with the claims of his native environment, the material to which he hopes to give poetic voice. Hartman's ideas, if not so much his terms, apply at least as well to the homecraft of the novel as to the romantic poetry that chiefly interests him. Novelists are certainly influenced by their predecessors. But they are usually also both quickened and challenged by the broader circumstances of a locality. In their customary enterprise of inventing a fictional world that represents the lived one in some fashion, novelists can be expected to be especially devoted to articulating the contingent materials of environment.

Hartman's purpose in linking tradition and locality is to establish a new sort of literary history, one genuinely both literary and historical. He calls for studying literary history from the writer's point of view, investigating how the writer's awareness of his own historicity affects his writing. This is my purpose also: the story of Faulkner's career is an internal history of how his works come into being. Indeed, some of the phases of Faulkner's career can be roughly defined by changes in the pressure exerted on him by tradition, locality, and also language. In Faulkner's poetry it is literary tradition that is the important and thus problematic constraint; in *Absalom, Absalom!* it is locality.

As Hartman suggests, the peculiar freedom of the writer

12. Geoffrey Hartman, "Towards Literary History," *Beyond Formalism* (New Haven 1970), 356–386.

and the particularity of his text arise from his being subject to several kinds of demands and several kinds of anxiety that do not coincide with one another. Attention to one constraint, rather than holding him in its spell, tends to raise questions about the others that then alter his relation to the first. The late romantic tradition in which Faulkner's poetry deliberately locates itself eventually leads him to serious questions about the capacity of language for visionary expression. These questions in turn become an explicit topic in one of Faulkner's early novels, *Mosquitoes,* and their resolution then leads to his first mature fiction, in which the visionary aesthetic with which he had begun is radically altered.

The striking feature of this process is how new work is built upon old. The career does not proceed as a linear development or a gradual evolution of its own latent tendencies. Rather it develops by expressly questioning the assumptions on which the earlier work depends. The new text is constructed in part as a criticism of an old one. The orderliness of this process of challenging the earlier work reflects the special discipline of the writer and of his career, a discipline which is considerably more specific than that of literature in general. This individual discipline thus functions within the various demands of wider literary exigencies and helps to organize the writer's response to them.

Because such discipline cannot be reduced either to the necessities of a collective structure or to the sovereignty of the individual writer, the study of it necessarily lies between poetics and exegesis. A writer's discipline is both peculiarly his own and yet potentially a far more rigorous limitation on him than those imposed by more global constraints. No writers have been less free than the most sophisticated and ambitious ones. No writers have adhered to an exacting discipline more assiduously than Flaubert and Conrad, to name two of the novelists against whom Faulkner avowedly measured himself.[13] The study of a literary career thus differs from poetics in its assumption that the making of a career, rather than being a passive, involuntary, or wittingly resigned implementation of what literature allows, is a production more fully the writer's own. It likewise differs from exegetical criticism in not positing some autonomous, originating figure who directs the career with complete freedom.

These methodological issues have a special importance for Faulkner criticism, because Faulkner is often given only grudging credit for any literary awareness, in spite of the recognized daring and complexity of his writings. He is likewise not normally thought of as a writer who has made a special discipline for himself out of the practice of literature. There are two reasons for this. One is that Faulkner criticism has generally restricted itself to explicating texts. Much of this commentary has been valuable, but it has tended to preclude the asking of larger questions. The second reason is that Faulkner's occasional public image as the gifted hick from Mississippi still makes us doubt his literary sophistication. The consequence is not that Faulkner's writing is disparaged, at least not any longer, but that he is thought to have been singularly free to warble his native wistaria notes wild.

My contention is that Faulkner's writing does conform to a discipline which both limits it and makes possible its particular character. This discipline can be most fully elucidated by studying how the career develops, but its signs are, of course, visible in individual texts, and some attention to these signs can be expected of any thorough reading of a text. A more detailed and exact consideration of the process already sketched, whereby new work builds upon and challenges the old, begins in fact with an attention to the enabling principles of the individual text. These are the spe-

13. "An Introduction for *The Sound and the Fury*," James B. Meriwether, ed., *Southern Review*, N.S. 8 (Autumn 1972), 708.

cific formal and thematic assumptions that make the text possible. They are, that is, the ideas about art and life which it was necessary for the writer to adopt, perhaps only provisionally or intuitively, to write that particular work. To search for the enabling principles of a work is to begin with the text and, with the aid of whatever other information is available, to work backward in order to reconstruct the theory that makes the text possible, a theory that may have no other manifestation than the practice represented in the text.[14]

In Faulkner's case at least, the search for the enabling principles of his works necessarily opens questions which can be answered only by studying the development of his career as well. The constitutive assumptions of texts produced at successive moments in his career prove to be closely related, so much so that later texts can be seen as specific responses to earlier ones and as reconsiderations of their enabling principles. Some assumptions continue to be maintained from one moment to the next, but others are specific challenges to the principles of an earlier text, challenges that are in fact anticipated or uncovered in the earlier text but not fully exploited by it.

An example which is worked out in detail in Chapter 4 is *As I Lay Dying*. That novel is one of Faulkner's most formally self-consistent texts, and quite specific enabling principles can be reconstructed for it. Moreover, these are held to with greater rigor and consistency than are those in most of Faulkner's other books. But the assumptions about language and about the writer's relationship to his fictional world which make *As I Lay Dying* possible are precisely the

14. In addition to the recently published *Selected Letters*, the chief sources of other information about the career are Faulkner's youthful essays and the interviews and classroom talks he gave late in life. These need to be used with some caution, but they are a more valuable resource than has sometimes been thought.

ones put in question by *Absalom, Absalom!*, the novel that represents the next distinct moment in Faulkner's career. In retrospect, the subsequent interrogation can be seen to be an extension of certain passages in *As I Lay Dying* itself. These passages already implicitly challenge the novel's enabling principles, but they are not so fully developed as to perform the thoroughgoing critique that *Absalom, Absalom!* accomplishes. Thus *As I Lay Dying* itself opens up the questions which then become explicit in a later text. In a similar though much less clean-edged manner, *Absalom, Absalom!* contains passages that raise questions about its own assumptions, questions taken up more fully in later texts.

Studying the enabling principles of one text thus leads directly to a study of the way successive texts or successive moments in the career are concatenated. Faulkner's writings manifest a particular kind of intertextuality among themselves, quite apart from the pertinent relationships they may have with texts by other writers. The exploitation of one set of assumptions within a given text raises up the challenge to these assumptions which becomes the basis of the next moment in the career. It is not that the individual works are incomplete or lacking in unity but that they disavow the illusion of self-sufficient completeness without on the other hand entirely dismantling themselves or failing to pursue what their enabling principles allow to be done. This concatenation of texts or groups of texts according to how they question their predecessors and make way for their successors is precisely the trajectory of Faulkner's career and the principle result of the kind of discipline to which it adheres.

Such discipline generates the coherence we will be primarily interested in, but a literary career can posess several sorts of coherence. These fall into two groups, each related to one meaning of the word "discipline." As an external regimen a discipline can be an organized body of knowledge and practice—a scholarly discipline, for example. Adherence to such a discipline is a commitment at least to begin by perpetuating its organization and working within its given set of rules and restraints. Let us call the corresponding regularity that a career may have its program. To study the program of a career is to emphasize unity, continuity, and preservation; often it is to show that the end is already implicit in the beginning or related to it by some organic analogy like blossom to seed or garden to individual plant.

A literary career that conforms to an explicit program inherited from past literary practices is a rare phenomenon, especially now, although the Virgilian tradition of a progression of forms from pastoral to epic was the career to which Pope still aspired. Much more common, especially among novelists, is the homemade program that the writer devises for himself, perhaps in mid-career as an affirmation of what he has already been doing and now resolves to perpetuate or consolidate. Multivolume works that dominate most of a writer's career, like those of Proust and Anthony Powell, exemplify one, often quite rigorous sort of program. Balzac's *Comédie Humaine* is the illustrious example of a less rigorously preordained kind of program that is both more common and more pertinent to Faulkner's work. Either of these programs binds together individual texts into something like a continuous whole.

The obvious program of this sort in Faulkner's career is his use of Yoknapatawpha County. There is little question that Faulkner fully intended Yoknapatawpha County to signify the larger whole in which most of his works were to be contained. He began cross-referencing characters and events from one text to another in the late 1920s, and by 1936 he was able to append a map of the county to one of his novels. Responding in 1955 to a question about the saga of Yoknapatawpha, Faulkner said that it was meant to give the body of his writing a structural unity analogous to the formal integrity of any individual work. "With *Soldiers' Pay*

[Faulkner's first novel] I found out writing could be fun. But I found out after that not only each book had to have a design but the whole output or sum of an artist's work had to have a design" (*LG* 255). Because Yoknapatawpha County is one aspect of Faulkner's career which has received a great deal of critical attention, nothing more need be said about it here except to distinguish it from the quite different coherence formed by the concatenation of successive texts and groups of texts.

No necessity other than the grim one of human mortality requires a program like Faulkner's (or Balzac's, on which it is consciously modeled) to come to a close. The writer may continue filling out his fictional cosmos to the end of his days. But just as Balzac in 1842 wrote a preface to his work which explicitly gathered it under a single rubric (and as Shakespeare is legendarily understood to have closed his career with Prospero's final words in *The Tempest*), so Faulkner planned to close off his writing with a "Doomsday Book, the Golden Book, of Yoknapatawpha County. Then I shall break the pencil and I'll have to stop" (*LG* 255). Such consolidation as Balzac effected and Faulkner intended is a way of placing boundaries on one's writing. It signals that the unity of the work is no longer open, no longer subject to change or reconstitution. Many of the most interesting things in Balzac's and Faulkner's writings lie outside these boundaries, of course. But the point I wish to make or at least prepare for is that the other aspect of Faulkner's career, its ongoing trajectory, specifically refuses such boundaries and such final unities. Rather than settling upon a design that may attain completion, it projects the perpetual reconstitution of new designs out of old ones.

This other aspect of career is one in which discipline is construed as disciplined behavior or as the self-regulation of a system. I borrow the model for this from cybernetics and communications theory and from their application to the

study of open systems.[15] The regularity of behavior in a
tidewater estuary or a corporation lies in the internal coherence of successive states of the system rather than in the
conformance to an external, unchanging program. Such a
system is capable of "reprogramming" itself at any point:
capable, that is, of remembering its own past, perceiving a
present environment, and using information derived from
both sources to plot a future course. Because any course of
action both modifies present conditions and alters the contents of memory, the system is guided by a continuous feedback loop that is the source of its discipline. In its broadest
form cybernetic theory offers a general model of goal-
seeking behavior in open systems. The course of a literary
career is certainly that, whatever important differences there
may be with systems in which feedback is an identifiable
mechanism and not a metaphor for an observable function-
ing. The relations that I mean to demonstrate between new
work and old in Faulkner's writing are the results of this
feedback function in his career. My emphasis, however, will
not be on what gets carried over through successive moments in the career. There are certain continuities in the career's trajectory, but they are generally much less intriguing
than the discontinuities that signal a change in program.

   Cybernetics likely suggests to some humanists the dark
regions of computer engineering or, worse, the chilling
technology of the electronic battlefield. These are indeed its
origins and its most deadly applications, but cybernetics is

15. For an introduction to cybernetics and the study of complex, open
systems, see either Donald M. Mackay, *Information, Mechanism, and Meaning* (Cambridge, Mass. 1969) or W. Ross Ashby, *An Introduction to Cybernetics,* 2nd ed. (London 1964). The critical and philosophical implications
of this field are most fully developed in Gregory Bateson's *Steps to an
Ecology of Mind* (New York 1972) and Anthony Wilden's *System and
Structure* (London 1972). In another context I have tried to summarize
some fundamental cybernetic ideas in parts 2 and 3 of "For a Cybernetics
of Reading," *Modern Language Notes,* 92 (December 1977), 945–968.

in fact a logic whose counterparts have long been employed by philosophers and historians under different names. Hegel's dialectic and Sartre's project are two well-known examples.[16] Moreover, cybernetic ideas ought to be capable of more extensive literary application than is made here. For example, I find that the significant patterns in Faulkner's career arise from formal and aesthetic issues of a kind familiar to what is often called intrinsic criticism. Such issues appear to be strikingly independent of other matters one might expect to be pertinent. A cybernetic approach, should however, be able to incorporate these other matters readily in cases where they are relevant. For instance, the concept of a career as an open, goal-seeking system would justify no a priori neglect of the circumstances of a writer's personal life. It would be foolish to discuss a career such as Yeats's without taking full account of his life. Likewise, for some writers the reception of their works plays an essential role. Melville's or Norman Mailer's awareness of his reputation and of the circulation of his books is surely an important

16. Leopold von Ranke's understanding of freedom and necessity supplies a close parallel to my argument about their operation in a literary career. "Let us admit that history can never have the unity of a philosophical system; but it is not without an inner continuity. Before us we see a range of successive events that condition one another. When I say 'condition,' I do not mean with absolute necessity. The great thing is, rather, that human freedom is involved everywhere. The writing of history follows the scenes of freedom. This is its greatest attraction. But freedom is combined with power, germinal power. Without the latter the former disappears, both in the events of the world and in the sphere of ideas. At every moment something new can begin, something whose sole origin is the primary and common source of all human activity. Nothing exists entirely for the sake of something else, nothing is entirely identical with the reality of something else. But there is still a deep inner unity present everywhere, of which no one is entirely independent. Beside freedom stands necessity. It consists in what has already been formed and cannot be destroyed, which is the basis of all new activity. What has already come into being constitutes the continuity with what is coming into being." Quoted by Hans-Georg Gadamer, *Truth and Method* (New York 1975), 180.

part of the "information input" that helps to determine the subsequent progress of the career. In Faulkner's case, however, especially after 1929, the principal continuities and discontinuities spring from the internal dynamics of the texts he writes.

The most important continuity in Faulkner's career is the conformity of his writing to a principle enunciated in a 1955 interview: "The aim of every artist is to arrest motion, which is life, by artificial means and hold it fixed so that 100 years later when a stranger looks at it, it moves again since it is life" (*LG* 253). In contrast to the continuities of Yoknapatawpha County, which include little more than subject matter, the concept of arrested motion implies specifications of method, form, theme, and purpose. Richard Adams was the first to show its significance in detail.[17] Drawing in part on earlier studies of Faulkner's style, Adams has demonstrated that images of arrested motion and situations in which the flux of time is suspended or frozen pervade Faulkner's work from first to last. He has also shown that the narrative method in several of Faulkner's major novels can be understood as a deliberate attempt to arrest and thereby manifest the turbulent flux of experience. Moreover, I think it can be argued that the enabling principles of texts written at different moments in Faulkner's career represent specific, detailed versions of the general understanding of art as arrested motion.

Nonetheless, if the concept of arrested motion gives us the most significant image for the overall coherence of Faulkner's writings and even an explicit paradigm for his art, it does not by itself supply an instrument for understanding his development. The concept is both too general and too ahistorical. Faulkner proclaims it not merely for his own work but for all art, and in fact the terms of the para-

17. Richard P. Adams, *Faulkner: Myth and Motion* (Princeton 1968).

digm are sufficiently broad that almost any work of art—certainly any that is at all representational—could be fitted to them without great distortion. Also, it is uncertain just when in Faulkner's writings before 1955 arrested motion might have attained the status of a paradigm, even an implicit or intuitive one. Although Faulkner may have understood his work in such terms at an early date, it seems more likely that the specific enabling principles and the local understandings evident in his texts were necessary prerequisites to the more encompassing paradigm. The paradigm accordingly seems to summarize and consolidate the practices in his texts rather than to generate them.

With the advantage of hindsight, we can nonetheless speak of the specific moments in Faulkner's career as if they were interpretations of the more general principle whose articulation postdates them. Among the ways in which arrested motion can be interpreted as a specific conception of the writer's task, of the work he means to produce, and of the world which the work will both represent and take its place in are the following.

(1) Arrested motion can be an image of the pure aesthetic state and the act of arresting motion a means of transcending the messy fluidity of life. Faulkner's poetry and much of his early fiction are written according to such assumptions.

(2) Motion can be the very source of significance and therefore the phenomenon that the writer seeks to approach and to hold fixed by artificial means. This is the chief enabling principle of Faulkner's first mature fiction.

(3) If the writer understands himself to be a part of the motion he writes about, his task may be the difficult one of trying to arrest motion from within. This is the art of *Absalom, Absalom!* and other works of the late 1930s.

(4) If art is understood to be only one among many cultural forms in which motion gets arrested, the artist may use

his art to evaluate all such forms, fictions, and social structures. Faulkner makes this his primary purpose in the 1940s and 1950s.

The concept thus allows for art as a vision of the transcendence of life, art as a representation of life's motion, art as a problematics of arresting, and art as a meta-form for investigating the value of cultural forms.

Other quite different ideas about art could doubtless be drawn from the paradigm; these four are, in the order given, brief descriptions of the principal moments in Faulkner's career. A more complete account of each of them and how they succeed one another will be given in subsequent chapters, but a few things can be said at the outset on Faulkner's ideas of how a career should develop. As my listing of the four moments is meant to suggest, no relentless logic demands that one must follow another. Nor is the end already latent in the beginning, as ought to be true of a fully programmatic career. The moments represent, instead, points on a trajectory which might well have traced a different course. Faulkner's career develops systematically, but it does so in the manner of an open system, one that always remains open to chance and contingency even as it then incorporates them into the system.

There are two aspects to Faulkner's understanding of how a new text ought to be related to its predecessors. One is the assumption that Faulkner shares with most writers of his era: the artist has an obligation to make it new. The "it" may remain the same, but the writer must try to render it in a different and better way than his precursors have done: "All artists, all writers, deal in the same truth because there's not very many different phases of it, and it has been said before, said marvelously so many times before, and it is not enough just to want to say that as good as it has been said." (*LG* 106). The writer must also attempt in each work to advance beyond what he himself has already accomplished. On such grounds one may, as Faulkner did, disparage Hemingway "because he had found out early in life what he could do and he stayed with that pattern" (*LG* 179). Each new work must aim to be the writer's definitive accomplishment. "He's got to tell all the truth in that one time because he may not have another chance. And he tried before and it wasn't quite good enough. This time he will try again to make it better" (*LG* 106–107). An extreme example of this attitude is Joyce, who in *Finnegans Wake* seems to attempt to write the last book, the one that will make all subsequent books unnecessary. Faulkner comes near to this attitude when he says that "it takes only one book to do it," the "one perfect book" that will constitute the "single urn or shape that you want to do" (*FU* 65).

More characteristically, however, Faulkner seeks to hold in abeyance the totalization Joyce seems to attempt and the perfection designated by Mallarmé as The Book. Faulkner's career is defined both by an infinite "dream of perfection" and by a finite intention to go on continually producing new texts (*LG* 238). The latter motive is related to two of Faulkner's most important themes, the idea of life as motion and the concern for a capacity to endure and prevail. Both themes suggest the value of being able to continue to act and to produce. The writer's career accordingly becomes the perpetuation of his writing as a continual process of change. The dream of perfection and of the one perfect book represent a finality and totalization whose attainment is always postponed as each new text fails to match the dream, thus allowing the career to have a future and making the production of new texts both posible and necessary. Faulkner has several times said flatly that "the only alternative to change and progress is death."[18] For the writer the

18. The quoted phrase is from *Faulkner in the University*, 151. See also pages 4, 271, and 277.

perpetuation of change in his writing, the perpetuation of a healthy career, is a stay against death. "If we ever did attain the dream, match the shape, scale that ultimate peak of perfection, nothing would remain but to jump off the other side of it into suicide" (*ESPL* 143).

The trajectory of Faulkner's career is thus shaped by three interrelated things: a practice of challenging the inadequacies of previous texts, a duty to change and advance, and a need to keep future possibilities open. Up to this point, I have perhaps made the career seem an easy or inevitable accomplishment. Faulkner had only, it may·appear, to locate the doubtful assumptions of his previous texts and invent means for exploring these doubts in order for his career to flourish as a coherent and self-perpetuating system. The matter is not that simple, of course. For one thing, the path of his career no more determines the whole of his writing than does the Yoknapatawpha design. More importantly, Faulkner knows only too well how precarious the career is. Just as his occasional rhetorical bravado about enduring and prevailing is qualified by a lifetime of attention in his fiction to how rare and unstable these capacities are, so the ability of his career to perpetuate itself and to maintain coherence is challenged by the characters' failures to do so with their lives. The characters' difficulties in going on at all implicate the writer's capacity to go on producing texts; their struggle to have a relationship to the past which is neither stifling nor inconsequential implicates the ongoing coherence of the writer's career.

The most obvious threat to a career is the silence that ends it. Faulkner's novels are filled with characters whose careers are broken off or end in silence, and these supply instructive analogies for a writing career. Wayne Hightower is haunted by an image of past glory which for most of *Light in August* cripples his ability to live at all. Quentin Compson despairs at what a poor and shameful thing his life would be if he were to continue living it. Flem Snopes in *The Mansion* discovers that he has exhausted the possibilities of his career, a career whose program has been dictated by what others deem worth having. There being nothing more to do, he waits patiently for his cousin Mink to murder him.

Two other threats to a career's coherence are the failure to advance upon one's own past and the inability to maintain the vital relation to the past that allows for a future. The first results in merely repeating one's past achievements or producing slightly different versions of them. Such repetition is what Faulkner criticizes in Hemingway. The second failure, which is caused by a more radical break with the past or a complete disregard of it, results in mere dispersion. One's texts become isolated productions strewn randomly in time; for this reason they have no power to breed consequences for themselves in the form of new work. Each new text must be a radically new beginning, and in Faulkner's fictional world such attempts to begin anew are always futile.

Repetition and dispersion often go together in Faulkner's novels. A number of characters (Quentin Compson, Joe Christmas, both Bayard Sartorises) are haunted by the difficulty of not repeating the past, and this is frequently a cause for their despair. A more apposite case is Thomas Sutpen, who believes he can begin anew but winds up instead repeating and perpetuating a system of injustice he had meant to repudiate. Ike McCaslin is more aware of the power of his inherited past than Sutpen, and he effects a more radical break with it. But in repudiating the McCaslin plantation, Ike also relinquishes a future. He finds himself isolated in the world and powerless to speak or act with any consequence. His eventual situation as a childless figure living on the fringes of his world is oddly like that of the fliers in *Pylon*, Faulkner's most striking representatives of dispersion. "There was really no place for them in the culture. . . . They had escaped the compulsion of accepting a past and a future, . . . they had no past. They were as ephemeral as the butterfly" (*FU* 36). Dispersion is for Faulkner virtually equivalent to ephemerality.

In Faulkner's world, to have a future and to be of consequence thus require a disciplined relationship with the past. To be merely a prisoner of one's past is to be powerless, like Quentin Compson. To have cut oneself off from it is to be adrift, like Linda Snopes Kohl at the end of *The Mansion.* The discipline that gives Faulkner's career its coherence is accordingly of paramount significance to him as a writer. It is what makes possible the career's very existence.

In addition to its significance for the writer, the career's coherence has special relevance for us as readers. For one thing, the career supplies a useful context for understanding individual works more fully. One can certainly read any of Faulkner's books without caring about its place in his development. But to do so risks obscuring some of the questions and issues to which the work addresses itself. Worse, it risks assuming the test to be a given thing, not a produced one. Viewing literary works as timeless aesthetic monuments, for example, often subtly relegates them to an ahistorical, nonhuman, and ultimately lifeless realm.

Second, the writer's career often supplies a considerable portion of the authority of his writing and hence of what we see in it as belonging to him as an author. For a text to gain in authority as the result of a writer's subsequent work is a common enough occurrence. Wallace Stevens's *Harmonium* was once widely and not without justification thought of as a dandy's exercise in verbal exuberance. But the volume gains considerably when the more demanding discipline that it also exhibits is sustained and advanced in subsequent texts. It is not that Stevens's early readers were blind; it is that the aspects of the poetry that get perpetuated or transformed become more significant because of such consequences. The phenomenon here is a sort of retroactive bestowal of authority and an *ex post facto* transformation of a writer's texts into an author's. Faulkner's poems exemplify a related phenomenon. They are quite undistinguished in themselves. Yet in their presentation of themes and images that Faulkner would later use more successfully and in their allegiance to an aesthetic that he would have to alter significantly in order to write his novels, the poems claim our attention. Indeed, the authority of the novels themselves is enhanced by an understanding of the path that Faulkner followed in order to reach the point of being able to write them.

2

Visionary Poetics

> I'm a failed poet. Maybe every
> novelist wanted to write poetry
> first.
>
> —*Lion in the Garden*, 238

Faulkner the apprentice poet is a very different sort of artist from Faulkner the master novelist. The poems he wrote between about 1915 and 1925 are strikingly unlike most of the later fiction in what they assume to be the essential purpose of literary art. The transition from poetry to prose that Faulkner made in the 1920s is thus anything but a natural or inconsequential change of genre. Indeed, the salient question for us about the poems is why Faulkner stopped writing them.

There are, to be sure, some conspicuous similarities between the poetry and the prose. We can, for example, notice Faulkner trying out in verse a number of themes and images that reappear in the later work, and we can also discover in the poetry several clues to the literary and intellectual background of the fiction. To read the poems primarily for the light they throw on the novels, however, would obscure the dynamics of Faulkner's career. In order to understand what encouraged him to give up writing poetry, we need to suspend our capacity for hindsight a little and see the poetry on its own terms. This in turn requires a more patient scrutiny of the poems than their comparatively slight intrinsic merit would justify. Indeed, it is the failure of the poetry—especially the thematic and compositional impasse at which it arrives—that establishes more than anything else the initial momentum of Faulkner's career.

Asked on his visit to Japan in 1955 to speak about his early interest in poetry, Faulkner distinguished sharply between the methods of the poet and those of the prose writer. His words are unpersuasive as a general principle, but they apply very well to his own work: "The poet deals with something which is so pure and so esoteric that you cannot say he is English or Japanese—he deals in something that is universal. That's the distinction I make between the prose writer and the poet, the novelist and the poet—that the poet deals in something universal, while the novelist deals in his own traditions" (*LG* 96). Faulkner's poems do disregard precisely those impurities that will dominate his fiction: social setting, historical context, interpersonal relationships, and in general the contingencies of a self's environment. In place of these the poems offer a solitary consciousness seeking to realize a visionary state. The state is usually associated with images of langour, Keatsian slow time, and arrested motion, as in the following lines from "Adolescence."

> Within this garden close, where afternoon
> To evening languishing, is like to swoon
> A Diana from her troubled draperies
> In carved escape, a slim arrested moon
> Across the tangled yew she has for screen
> Gazes on the stagnant lilied green
> Of water. [UVa][1]

1. Poems quoted from manuscript will be cited parenthetically according to the library in which they may be found: the Alderman Library of the University of Virginia (UVa), the Humanities Research Center of the University of Texas at Austin (UT), and the Berg Collection of the New York Public Library (NYPL). "Adolescence" can also be found in the *Phoenix Book Shop Catalog* #100 (Fall 1971), 10. Other manuscript poems reproduced or transcribed in bibliographic materials will be identified in footnotes. The most complete listing of Faulkner's poems is Keen

As a poet Faulkner works directly with what he believes to be pure universals, that is, timeless, esoteric states that may bear scant resemblance to the circumstances of life around him. As a mature novelist, he pursues the more tangled significance of the finite cultural tradition in which he finds himself. (The real difference, we shall come to see, lies not strictly between poetry and prose but between visionary art and the mode that eventually replaces it.)

His use of the word "traditions" should not mislead us. It refers to the particularities of social history rather than to the global company of pure and esoteric poets. Faulkner starts out working in a definite poetic tradition. Like the later moments in the career, the beginning thus stands in deliberate relation to a past from which it has proceeded and a future in which it expects to continue. Faulkner's poems clearly mean to belong to a literary movement that has an established and honorable past. They mean also to be decidedly modern and even to belong to what he considered the avant-garde of American poetry in the 1910s.

The widest tradition upon which Faulkner's verse depends is the visionary wing of romanticism. Like his predecessors, Faulkner wants to constitute in his poetry a transcendent realm from which all worldliness and impurity have been purged. More specifically, Faulkner's poems appear near the close of the most recent distinctive episode in this tradition. The episode can be called the symbolist movement, provided that this shorthand term is understood not in a narrow sense but as a name for the general continuity of most deliberately avant-garde French and English poetry from Mallarmé to early T.S. Eliot. It thus includes the *symbolistes,* the decadents and aesthetes of the 1890s, and

---

Butterworth's "Census of Manuscripts and Typescripts of William Faulkner's Poetry," *A Faulkner Miscellany,* James B. Meriwether, ed. (Jackson, Miss. 1974), 70–97. This includes two pages of addenda to the original "Census" in the Summer 1973 issue of *Mississippi Quarterly.*

most of the early modernists. Faulkner's place within this movement is that of a minor poet who never really establishes a distinctive voice of his own. The reader encountering his poetry for the first time is in fact likely to be struck by how familiar it sounds. Echoes, derivations, and outright borrowings from such poets as Swinburne, Verlaine, Housman, Pound, and Eliot abound in Faulkner's verse.

To pursue the origins of Faulkner's poetry would be to map its affinities with an entire range of aesthetic ideas and stylistic predilections jointly held by numerous poets writing between 1870 and 1920. Yet a meticulous hunt for sources would be rather beside the point in comparison to the massive influence of an entire tradition. For example, Faulkner entitled his first published poem "L'Apres-Midi d'un Faune," and it bears some resemblance to Mallarmé's eclogue. The extent of Faulkner's familiarity with Mallarmé is not otherwise known, however, and the title may well have come by way of Debussy. In either case, Faulkner had by an early age incorporated enough of the visionary tradition to be quite capable of reproducing the dreaminess of Mallarmé's poem on his own.

In spite of Faulkner's obvious awareness of a great deal of recent and contemporary symbolist poetry, his own work is not particularly up-to-date. He wrote most of the poems at a time when the *fin-de-siècle* style he generally preferred was giving way to the sparer modernism that for us names the difference between Swinburne and Pound. Faulkner really becomes a modernist only in his fiction. Nevertheless, the poetic tradition he follows is as important to the directions he pursued in the novel as, say, Yeats's Celtic Twilight poems are to his later verse. On the one hand, Faulkner's shift from poetry to fiction is the sharpest break in his career. Several aspects of his mature fiction can in fact best be understood as a deliberate rejection of the aesthetic stance adopted in the poetry. On the other hand, there are a number of prominent continuities between the poetry and the fiction, most of them related to the continuing hold upon his imagination of the concept of arrested motion. Quentin Compson, for example, is clearly an avatar of the speakers in many of Faulkner's poems. His yearning for a transcendent state of arrested motion clearly derives from theirs.

Arrested motion is rarely an image of the artwork or the artist's task at the beginning of Faulkner's career. From the outset, however, it explicitly represents the visionary state, the artist's goal. Arrested motion is thus a theme before it becomes a method, and in the poetry it is an even more pervasive theme than in the fiction. Most of the poems are primarily motivated by a quest for the fusion of temporality and eternity. An "orisoned music" that "suspends the uncompleted birth / And death of day and night" is exactly the universal purity the poetry seeks to constitute ("Drowning," NYPL).

So dominant is the quest for a state of arrested motion that we should read the poetry more as a continual meditation on a single theme than a series of discrete works.[2] Almost all the speakers in the poetry express the same desire. They long not for an object or even quite for a concrete state of being, but for the transcendence that one poem frankly calls the "absolute" (untitled fragment, UT). The

2. Faulkner seems himself to have held the integrity of single poems in slight regard. He continually recycled images, lines, and whole stanzas from one poem to another. This impression is enhanced by what has happened to the extant manuscripts. Many of them survived a fire only in charred, fragmentary, and shuffled form. One thus cannot always discriminate among drafts, fragments, and completed works or confidently establish a "best text." Nevertheless, it is necessary to rely extensively on the manuscripts in order to reconstruct Faulkner's poetic practices. Most of the poems he did publish were chosen and revised after he had largely abandoned writing poetry. The versions in *A Green Bough* (1933), for example, sometimes reflect the rather different point of view he had attained as a novelist. So also do the selections for that volume; several important poems were omitted, and these still exist only in manuscript.

conditions of this absolute include the immersion in an ideal fullness of being, the permanent and total presence of world to self, and the fusion of time and eternity.

The absolute is usually experienced and also represented negatively as an absence that nonetheless calls out to the self. Faulkner's poems often depict a lone self in or against a highly stylized pastoral scene, like those in *The Marble Faun*. It is the scene that awakens the self's awareness of the absent ideal. Sometimes the landscape shares in the melancholic "cold old sorrow of the world" (UVa).[3] At other times nature is merely an occasion for the self's yearnings, and the sorrow is the more intense for being unshared. In either case, the landscape itself is the primary symbol of the absolute or rather of its absence.

Faulkner's symbolic landscapes belong to a specifically poetic realm, a place where one may expect to find purity and universality. This is most obviously true of the many poems in which mythological beings appear. It is true as well even of the ones that seem to describe a more or less realistic scene. For example, the peaceful landscape whose features are catalogued in "April" is not placed before us as an object of perception or contemplation. The beginning of each stanza carefully locates the scene in a "somewhere" that lies beyond perception and can presumably only be reached by an act of vision.[4]

Sometimes the melancholy awakened by such landscapes is associated, as one might expect, with the bleakness of winter or fall. The barren, often rainy landscape then plays a "sad and silver music" beneath which the poet can at times hear the "richer chord" of a desired fullness ("Cathedral in Rain," UT). Most of the poems are set in spring or sum-

3. A typescript of this untitled poem is reproduced in *William Faulkner: "Man Working," 1919–1962,* Linton R. Massey, compiler (Charlottesville, Va. 1968), 77.

4. *Contempo,* 1 (February 1, 1932), 1.

mer, however, and they present scenes that are meant to signify the beautiful. The prologue to *The Marble Faun* is typical of Faulkner's landscapes: slender poplars moving lightly in the breeze and overlooking a calm pool that surrounds a silver fountain. When the landscape is not a formal garden, it is usually a sheltered grove in the woods—cool, shady, and above all, quiet. Such cultivated, formalized natural beauty presents a momentary calm that evokes the poet's desire for a gently swaying eternal stillness.

It is the particular power of natural beauty in April and May to arouse visionary longing, because such beauty always carries with it signs of its own transitoriness. The poet rarely perceives only the immediate splendor of the scene. Sometimes he envisions the landscape as a further movement in an ancient dance of bloomings and dyings.

> Poplar leaves swirl sunward, bright with rime,
> To a stately minuet of wind in wheat;
> And spring is blown on ruins of old time,
> Cruel, incurious, superbly sweet. [5]

At other times the landscape manifests the abiding impersonality of nature, and the dance becomes man's futile, evanescent attempt to join in its rhythms.

> But the clear brown whisper of rain in woods of April
> And the grave sweet slant of rain in April leaves
> Cradled a dance that will not be danced tomorrow,
> And a bending of grass that tomorrow bends and heaves
>   .   .   .
> Then another dance is only a sleep and a vision
> To the twitched cords of the brain and heart of a man
> And sinister hands of sun sweep moor and barren
> Where sheep have cropped the pastures of old Pan. [6]

Spring itself is less a welcome return of life and warmth than a marauder, bringing awareness of desire and of the

5. "I Will Not Weep for Youth," *Contempo*, 1 (February 1, 1932), 1.
6. "The Flowers That Died," *Contempo*, 3 (June 25, 1933), 1.

necessity of change to a world that had seemed to escape them for a season. In "Adolescence" spring is the barbarian who "pillages and sacks this ancient close," destroying the "citadel" of peaceful oblivion (UVa).

The beautiful landscape is thus not itself the object of desire but the figure of a purer, more esoteric desire. Its function in the poems is that explicitly given to the calls of the wild geese in poem XXVIII of *A Green Bough*. The geese are "seeking some high desire" by flying "over the world's rim"—beyond the limits of what is possible in the landscape of "bland November." Their "lonely voices" awaken poetic vision, which here is also the poet's memory of "this dust ere 'twas flesh." Just as the geese are imagined to be drawn onward by a sound only they can hear, so the poet is drawn by a "sharp unease" of the blood, which recalls something that was its own but has been lost. The geese, then, are both the stimulus of the poet's reawakened desire and a model for it, since they also seek to exceed the limits of the natural world.

In addition to landscape, there are several other important images of such desire in Faulkner's poetry. One is the imagery of music and dance, prominent in several of the poems already cited. Another is the nymphlike maiden, whose beauty resembles that of the trees and fountains of the scene in which she is normally placed: "Slender like a boy she was, and slight / And silver as a fountain's jet" (untitled fragment, UT). (In Faulkner's first two novels she will reappear—in Cecily Saunders and Patricia Robyn—as the slim-hipped coquette who represents Faulkner's version of the modern young woman of the 1920s.) Unlike other images, the woman is sometimes an object of desire in and of herself. Several poems present either songs of seduction or recollections of momentary sexual bliss. But in the mythological poems, where the figure is actually a nymph, sexual desire is clearly a metaphor for something beyond itself. In

such poems fulfillment of sexual desire is either a pure ec-
stasy never to be achieved or an event whose attainment
discloses a purer, unattainable desire beyond.

The most important symbol other than the landscape is
the faun. The faun exists in a middle state, between the
human and the fully divine, and can thus serve as an exemplary figure of desire for the absolute. *The Marble Faun* is
the most detailed exposition of this theme. The statue of the
faun is, after a fashion, eternal and hence barred from life.
Awakened by Pan's pipes, the faun wants first to break his
"marble bonds" and become one of those who can "fade
and fall" (*MF,* 12, 31). But when he does come to life (or
imagines he does), almost immediately he longs to return to
the initial "sun-drenched revery" so that "the nameless pain
/ To fuller live and know again / No more will send me over
earth" (*MF* 11, 18–19). The poem is structured by a series
of oscillations between the desire for "quietude and rest,"
symbolized at one point by the statue in a snow-filled garden, and the yearning for vitality that sends the faun racing
through spring and summer landscapes. Neither state is satisfactory without the other, but the faun discovers he cannot
exist in both at once. At the end he laments in comparing
his situation as a marble figure which dreams of "things I
know yet cannot know" to that of the insentient walls of his
garden:

> They do not know nor care to know,
> Why evening waters sigh in flow;
> .   .   .
> Nor why the seasons, springward wheeling,
> Set the bells of living pealing.
> They sorrow not that they are dumb:
> For they would not a god become.   [*MF,* 48]

The faun's longing for divinity expresses the metaphysical
character of his desire quite directly. He wants not merely
to satisfy his desires but to surpass them, to achieve a divine

fullness of being in which no ache of longing can arise. Likewise, in "The Faun," apparently a much later poem, the title figure also wants to be fully a god and "from a cup unlipped, undreamt, unguessed, / Sip that wine sweetsunned for Jove's delight" (*EPP* 119). Other poems express this yearning for absolute being more obliquely. In poem XXV of *A Green Bough,* for example, in which the poet's dream is of both a woman and a landscape and yet of neither, desire is an abiding state that transcends the longing for any particular object.

Throughout Faulkner's poetry the absolute lies beyond any finite object of desire and even beyond anything the poet can envision concretely. Although it can be named as the "bright immutable beauty" of a landscape in arrested motion, it is named only as what is absent (untitled fragment, UT). The brightness is always dimmed by spatial or imaginative distance, and the immutable beauty proves in fact to be vulnerable to time, change, and decay. The oxymoronic images of arrested motion thus serve to express an impossible ideal more than a transcendent state the poet actually hopes to achieve. Although the desire for the absolute arises with each new spring, each new beloved, and every further note of Pan's pipes, the poet soon learns that the state can never be attained.

Two possibilities remain when the poet discovers that metaphysical desire cannot be fulfilled. One is to renounce such desire. Most of the poems Faulkner wrote in the style of A. E. Housman do just that. The other possibility is the desire for a state of peaceful oblivion that will put an end to all desiring. In several poems the speaker is an old man thankful for the waning of desire with age and looking forward to death as a time at which he can be completely indifferent to the return of spring.

> Death and I'll amicably wrangle, face to face
> Mouthing dried crumbs of pains and ecstasies

Regarding without alarm cold seas of space—
Eternity is simple where sunlight is.[7]

A few such poems follow Thomas Hardy's example in actually locating the contented speakers beyond the grave. Others portray life as a painful and unnecessary interruption of the happy state on the other side of birth and death.

Once there was a lightless time: I had not birth
—Be still, my heart, be still: you break in vain:
A shattered urn in wild and bitter earth—
There was beauty then, grief and pain
But I lay close and dark and richly dearth.
Why did I wake? When shall I sleep again?[8]

Nonetheless, the release from desire is not always clearly distinct from its fulfillment. If desire is the lack of the absolute, then the end of desire—in both senses of the phrase—will be the absolute itself. At the extreme, death becomes the primary object of longing. And in fact the two desirable states most often named in the poems are death and sleep, when one's longings have been extinguished or at least have disappeared for a while. Pan's final bestowal on the marble faun is the precious "gift of sleep" (*MF* 49). In "Adolescence" the poet seeks to remain "forever locked in sleep, when spring again / Returns to storm these ancient walls" (UVa). In one mythological poem Helen hopes to curb the sexual fury of the Centaur and be able to find a "beauty true and passionate" in calm union with him; but the "islanded repose" she dreams of proves to be the "undoubtful sleep" of death ("Helen and the Centaur," UT). Even in "Hymn," the single most exuberant and joyous of Faulkner's poems,

7. "I Will Not Weep for Youth," *Contempo,* 1 (February 1, 1932), 1.
8. "Admonishes His Heart," quoted from the private archives of Jill Faulkner Summers by Joseph Blotner, *Faulkner: A Biography* (New York 1977), I, 544.

beauty is to be sought "between sleep, sister of death . . . and death, brother of sleep" (UVa).[9]

The most voluptuous image of the desired state, an image that recurs in the fiction, is death by drowning. Much in the way Quentin Compson imagines it in *The Sound and the Fury*, a watery grave represents a place where the fulfillment and the extinction of desire meet in complete, lovely finality. Poem XIX of *A Green Bough*, for instance, is the nearest of all Faulkner's verses to a portrait of desire fulfilled.

> Within these slow cathedralled corridors
> Where ribs of sunlight drown
> He joins in green caressing wars
> With seamaids red and brown
>
> And chooses one to bed upon
> And lapped and lulled is he
> By dimdissolving music of the sun
> Requiemed down through the sea.

Such fulfillment presents Faulkner with a thematic impasse, however. On one hand is a wish for the release from desire that comes with old age and dying. On the other hand and only barely distinguishable from such a wish is the still potent dream of an absolute. But the dream is now fully recognized as a desire for death. "Know you not that when once you have wrought / The absolute, then you can only die?" (untitled fragment, UT). The poetry closes out its own possibilities of continuing shortly after it has begun. Consciousness seeks the absence of consciousness in death. And Faulkner's career as a poet, because it is founded on the necessity of both consciousness and the absolute, can only repeat the truth of their incompatibility.

9. "Hymn" is transcribed in *Man Collecting: Manuscripts and Printed Works of William Faulkner in the University of Virginia Library*, Joan StC. Crane and Ann E. H. Freudenberg, compilers (Charlottesville, Va. 1975), 126–127.

The thematic impasse is accompanied by a stalemate in the poetic theory underlying Faulkner's practice. We can best understand Faulkner's visionary poetics by first generalizing the preoccupation with landscape into a more inclusive mental topography. The individual poems almost always posit one realm against another, absent one; in the poetry as a whole, three different realms can be discerned. The least common is an ordinary world of rude circumstance and particularity. Most often it is portrayed satirically in styles deriving either from E. E. Cummings or from the Eliot of *Prufrock and Other Observations*. The quotidian world serves primarily as a contrast to a second, more idealized world. The second realm we may call, to borrow and somewhat alter the context of Richard Poirier's phrase, a world elsewhere. This is the poetic realm, where Faulkner's fauns and nymphs frolic among trees and fountains. The third realm is the absolute, the place where desire ceases. It is identified, as we have seen, with sleep and death and also with a faraway, changeless beauty.

Faulkner's chief means for establishing the poetic realm are the conventions of pastoral verse. Traditionally, of course, the pastoral is a world elsewhere, a realm of stylized simplicity set against the entanglements of city or court. Sometimes it is meant to be a version of actual, recognizable rural life. More often it is a world constructed in allegiance to specifically literary traditions. Faulkner's pastoral is decidedly of the latter kind. His landscapes populated with shepherds, fauns, and nightingales and blooming in gorse, heather, and hawthorne are set far from the American South. Most often the scenes are vaguely English, Italian, and Greek, but before all they are deliberately the landscapes of poetry.[10] The patently derivative quality of Faulkner's poetry is in this sense

10. Cleanth Brooks points this out also and lists a number of other non-Southern flora and fauna in "Faulkner as Poet," *Southern Literary Journal,* 1 (Autumn 1968), 5–19.

at least quite intentional. Borrowed images and lines and styles, carrying with them a secondhand literary prestige, help to signify the poetic as a distinct realm.

Poirier's exemplary writers—Faulkner the novelist among them—have to struggle free from the restrictions of an actual locality in order for style to do its magical work in creating an alternative world.[11] In his poetry, however, Faulkner presents such a world ready-made. Poetry, in its allegiance to esoteric purity, can leave behind the contingencies that fiction must deal with and perhaps transform. The poetic realm's status as an ideal alternative is equivocal, however. We can see this in the double use Faulkner makes of traditional pastoral figures like fauns and nymphs. To those nonvisionary souls who dwell in the ordinary world, the figures represent achieved desire. In "Eunice," for example, the speaker wonders if the girl had been seeking an ideal world of "fauns and nymphs in formal ways" (UVa). To the laborer in poem X the figures likewise represent both immortality and exuberant life: "Nymph and faun in this dusk might riot / Beyond all oceaned Time's cold greenish bar" (GB 30). But in other poems, as we have seen, the faun belongs only to the second realm, serving merely as a being in whom the longing for a purer transcendence is especially strong.

The fundamental relation in Faulkner's poetry is between the absolute and the poetic. The poetic may be a purification of the ordinary world, but it is not an end in itself. As in other varieties of symbolist poetry, the world of particularity is left behind for a poetic realm that must itself be transcended. The pastoral landscape as a whole is, in effect, a "symbol" of the absolute, but a symbol that always confesses the absence of what it symbolizes. Thus it seeks to efface itself before a dimly perceived purity that it can never represent adequately. Similar abnegations of the symbol to

11. Richard Poirier, *A World Elsewhere* (New York 1966).

something beyond its concrete referent occur in Yeats's early use of occult lore and in Mallarmé's complex syntax of negation. The poetic realm's deference to the absolute can be seen clearly in Faulkner's first published poem, one of the very few that attempts to depict a realm beyond the pastoral world elsewhere. In the first half of "L'Apres-Midi d'un Faune" the faun pursues his nymph through a cloudy landscape of desire until at last he possesses her. But he is himself then possessed by "a nameless wish to go / To some far silent midnight noon" (*EPP* 39). The fulfillment of his desire within the already mythological world requires the faun to discover the insufficiency of that world's objects of desire and to recognize in himself a metaphysical desire for the absolute. Nymph and landscape, Faulkner's usual symbols of desire, are left behind, and the faun dreams of a world beyond his own where ghostly figures dance beneath the moon.

The chief task of Faulkner's poetry is to express a poetic landscape in such a way that it will point beyond itself to the absolute. But here the topographical metaphor reveals its limitations, for the absolute cannot be a realm, if realm be thought of as divisible into parts or containing discrete features. As the locus of desire's end, it must be an indivisible plenum, for division would open a new space in which desire could reappear. The poetic realm in contrast is eminently differentiated, and each of its discrete features—trees, fountains, nymphs—possesses its own proper identity. The poetic realm can, in other words, be articulated, in the sense both of being segmented and of being uttered. Yet articulation can only be a deceptive, regrettable, but nonetheless inevitable property if the poetic realm is adequately to symbolize the absolute. What ought to point beyond itself to the absolute is not one or another feature of the landscape but the scene as a whole. Faulkner's poetics must then be one of creating poems as single, complex symbols whose articulated features disappear in the face of the seamless absolute they seek to express.

This amounts to saying that a poem must be an articulation of the inarticulable. The requirement corresponds to the thematic discovery of death as the end of metaphysical desire. It is another form of the impasse that limits the space in which truly pure and esoteric poetry can come into being. Once the tawdry, fragmentary world of particularity has been left behind, one symbol is about as effective in its inefficacy as any other. All poems become repetitions of the same poem. All are restricted to a narrow, one-dimensional space, an approach to the absolute and a falling back at the renewed discovery that it cannot be reached or expressed.

This, then, is why Faulkner comes to believe he is a failed poet. Quite apart from any considerations of the skill with which the poetry is written, it fails internally, on its own terms, because Faulkner is unable to enlarge the space in which it appears or to find some other roomier aesthetic space. The poet himself has only a narrow twilight corridor in which to dwell, between the scorned realm of particularity and the unattainable realm of the absolute. Hence the figure in poem XX, whom an earlier, longer version explicitly identifies as Orpheus, the traditional prototype of the visionary poet:

> Here he stands, while eternal evening falls
> And it is like a dream between gray walls
> Slowly falling, slowly falling
> Between two walls of gray and topless stone,
>   . . .
> Here he stands, without the gate of stone
> Between two walls with silence on them grown,
> And littered leaves of silence on the floor;
> Here, in a solemn silver of ruined springs
> Among the smooth green buds, before the door
> He stands and sings.   [GB 42]

Such a poet is not the active "carpenter" who assembles
Faulkner's novels but a passive, nearly immobile genius
possessed by the "divine fire" of poetic vision (*FU* 117,
280). He is also not necessarily even a poet, in the strict
sense of one who writes verse. Faulkner's distinction between the poet and the prose writer refers to differences in
intention and method rather than in form. Faulkner can
thus expressly and plausibly identify a prose tale such as
"Carcassonne" as the work of the poet in him (*FU* 22).
That story seems as well to be an allegorical portrait of the
visionary artist. Its protagonist, lying cramped and mo-
tionless underneath a strip of tarred roofing paper in his
shabby garret apartment, dreams of performing *"something
bold and tragical and austere"* (*CS* 899). He is a writer of
poetry apparently only in the imagination of his landlady,
for he scorns the "allocutions of stealthful voracity" that he
associates with Byron and also with the rats who scurry
about his dark attic (898). His vision, set against the recurrent motif of a watery grave in the "windless gardens of
the sea," is to ride a buckskin pony *"right off into the high
heaven of the world"* (899). In this way he will become like
the valiant Norman horse who charged on through enemy
ranks though cut in two by a Saracen blade and already
dead. The *"blue electricity"* of the pony's eyes is like the fire
of poetic inspiration, but as in Faulkner's verse the protagonist's dream goes beyond a merely poetic or heroic
state to the "blue precipice never gained," which is transcendence and death (895).

The heavenly horizon sought in "Carcassonne" is literally
air and airiness. Even during his visionary phase Faulkner
was not wholly without misgivings about how easily such
an art could become too ethereal. In a 1925 essay he pointedly compares the modern poets' vain attempts at "spiritual
beauty" with the work of Keats and Shakespeare; these two,
he asserts, have been able to achieve such visionary beauty

in their poetry, "yet beneath it one knows are entrails; masculinity" (*EPP* 117).

Most of the poems Faulkner wrote under the influence of
Housman's *A Shropshire Lad* reflect a similar uneasiness
about venturing so far into airy realms at the expense of the
plowman's earth and the "brow of time" (*GB* 55). These
poems denounce all yearning for the absolute and call nos-
talgically for return to a life in which desire remains simple
and nonmetaphysical. Poems VII, VIII, and IX of *A Green
Bough* each proclaim the futility of all high desire and the
"furious emptiness of all strife." The exemplary figure is the
stolid plowman who, indifferent to the "golden madness"
of the mockingbird's song and the "pageantry" of "warriors
long ago," finds "but simple scents and sounds; / And this is
all, and this is best" (*GB* 29).

The stark ironies of such poems and their high valuation of
the "splendor of fortitude" contrast markedly with the visionary yearnings of Faulkner's other poetry (*EPP* 117).
These poems are closer in spirit to the fiction Faulkner came
to write after 1929 than to the other poems with which they
are contemporary. The Housman-like poems in fact make up
a greater proportion of the lyrics collected in the 1933 *Green
Bough* than they do among all of Faulkner's extant verse. This
seems to reflect their greater compatibility with the novels
Faulkner was writing when he made the final selections and
revisions for that volume. I at least cannot perceive any no-
ticeable superiority in such poems over uncollected ones like
"Helen and the Centaur," "Hymn," and "Aubade."

The criticism that the Housman-like poems make of the
visionary impulse is carried on by much of Faulkner's fiction. However, the abandonment of poetry for fiction did
not itself immediately entail so decided a renunciation of
metaphysical desire as can be observed in these poems. By
the 1930s such desire is treated with a good deal of fasci-
nated skepticism. But in the years up to and including the

writing of *The Sound and the Fury* in 1928, Faulkner was undergoing a second apprenticeship at the craft of fiction. The novels written during this period resemble the visionary poems more than the Housman-like ones in most respects. *The Sound and the Fury* itself can from one point of view be understood as the culmination of Faulkner's visionary poetics. From another, equally essential point of view, however, *The Sound and the Fury* inaugurates the initial phase of Faulkner's mature fiction and in so doing renounces a visionary aesthetic.

The visionary impulse never entirely disappears from Faulkner's work. The impasse reached by his poetry points him toward a kind of fiction that opens the questions about the particular and the ordinary which his poems had closed at the outset. But the dream of a transcendent absolute persists in a curious way, as an ideal that haunts the writer even when he is fully aware that its attainment is not only impossible but not even desirable. It is in this way that I think we can best understand Faulkner's frequent and well-known assertions that every one of his books is a failure. His insistence that all of his novels fail to "reach the unattainable dream" indicates a good bit more than artistic modesty and more also than the inspired perversity Walter Slatoff has seen in it (*FU* 207).[12]

The statements about failure were most often provoked by Faulkner's attempt to explain the rankings of contemporary novelists he had unguardedly made in a 1947 classroom talk. Several such statements go on to include a reflection on his own abandoning of poetry for fiction. The double context is significant; failure means the same thing in both. Failure results not from "the value of the work, the impact or perfection of its own kind that it had," but from a reluctance to commit oneself unreservedly to the "dream of per-

12. Walter Slatoff, *Quest for Failure* (Ithaca, N.Y. 1960).

fection," to the absolute as it is envisioned in Faulkner's poetry (*LG* 82). Thus the "finest failure" among his novels is *The Sound and the Fury*, the book which is most directed toward that visionary absolute but which also first establishes the method of Faulkner's fiction and thus sets his career on a course away from esoteric purity (*LG* 92).

Faulkner's career as a novelist depends in fact on a principled failure to satisfy the requirements of visionary art. Having arrived in one genre at the impasse of a longing for death, Faulkner understood well that the capacity to maintain a career, to go on writing, depends on such failure.

> If I could write all my work again, I am convinced that I would do it better, which is the healthiest condition for an artist. That's why he keeps on working, trying again; he believes each time and this time he will do it, bring it off. Of course he won't, which is why this condition is healthy. Once he did it, once he matched the work to the image, the dream, nothing would remain but to cut his throat, jump off the other side of that pinnacle of cut perfection into suicide.   [*LG* 238]

The matter was doubtless not so clear in 1925, when Faulkner began writing fiction seriously, and probably at no time was it quite so melodramatic as his rhetoric makes it sound. But the need to find an alternative to the suicidal longings of the visionary poet and to create an artistic space that makes room for life is certainly what empowers Faulkner's search for a new artistic method in the late 1920s.

3

The Search for a Narrative Method

The completion of *The Sound and the Fury* in 1929 is the most dramatic turning point in Faulkner's career. The book marks the beginning of his artistic maturity and the end of a lengthy double apprenticeship, first as a poet and then as a novelist. Moreover, it inaugurates the artistic method he will continue to use and develop for the next three decades. Faulkner discovers for the first time in the novel a way of selecting, organizing, and representing his literary materials that is fully compatible with the demands of prose narrative. Still, *The Sound and the Fury* remains a transitional work in some ways. In spite of its clear superiority over Faulkner's previous writings, it looks back to the poetry and the apprentice fiction just as much as it anticipates the subsequent major novels. Two divergent conceptions of art confront each other in the book. One is the art of the visionary poet, dreaming of a timeless realm of purity and finding his antecedents among the romantic poets. The other is the art of the realistic novel, broadly defined, and its creator is concerned with the fate of such dreams in a concrete historical environment. He finds his antecedents in the classic novelists of the nineteenth century and in the demonstration by such contemporaries as

Joyce and Eliot of new possibilities for the objective representation of deeply personal themes.

Our question is how Faulkner moves from one conception to the other. This in turn requires a close examination of the narrative methods sanctioned by each, for it is Faulkner's discovery of a suitable method that most immediately gives rise to the new conception of his artistic goals.

The shift epitomized by *The Sound and the Fury's* double allegiance is accompanied by at least three other large changes in Faulkner's work. Each of these has some claim to be considered the decisive factor in Faulkner's search for a method. The first is a change in his literary materials. Faulkner himself emphasized the importance of this in a 1955 interview, comparing the discovery that his "little postage stamp of native soil was worth writing about" to the opening of a gold mine (*LG* 255). The second is a changed appreciation of the novel as a genre. It results not from his discerning a subtle, previously hidden potential in the genre but from committing himself to its most basic and even obvious characteristics, such as a story involving some form of human conflict. The third is an altered understanding of arrested motion. Before 1929, Faulkner usually stressed the result, arrested motion as a static image of transcendence. In *The Sound and the Fury* he stresses the process, the activity of the writer (and the characters) in arresting motion. Among other things, this gives him an artistic principle more readily compatible with the necessarily temporal structure of narrative.

The first of these changes, the invention of Yoknapatawpha County, is obviously crucial to Faulkner's development, but it seems to me less telling than the other two. Faulkner's initial belief, as reported some years later to Malcolm Cowley, was that a novel should deal with entirely imaginary scenes and people.[1] The belief appears to have

1. Malcolm Cowley, *The Faulkner-Cowley File* (New York 1966), 109.

contributed to the arty, overly contrived depiction of setting and character in Faulkner's first novel. Certainly, the use of familiar, local materials in the third novel and in the manuscript fragment entitled "Father Abraham" helps Faulkner to avoid such artifice; it also supplies a dense social and historical context of the kind that is sorely lacking in the two earlier novels, *Soldiers' Pay* (1926) and *Mosquitoes* (1927). Both in the 1929 version entitled *Sartoris* and in Douglas Day's reconstruction of the original *Flags in the Dust,* the third novel is actually more diffuse and awkward than its predecessors. Selecting congenial materials is at best only an initial step toward finding a satisfactory means of representing their artistic significance.

In a preface composed for a never-published edition of *The Sound and the Fury,* Faulkner expressly links the advance represented by that book to a new appreciation of its genre. The appreciation is a consequence of writing the book, however, not a prior condition. Only after completing the novel, Faulkner writes in 1933, did he learn how to read— retroactively and without opening a volume—the novelists he had devoured as a youth: Balzac, Conrad, Flaubert, Dostoevski, and James. Only then did he realize that there was something identifiably and distinctively novelistic "to which the shabby term Art not only can, but must, be applied."[2] The capital letter here is especially revealing, for above all else in the 1920s Faulkner meant his own work to be Art. Moreover, his earliest ideas about what high art should be largely rule out the usual enabling premises of the novel.

In Faulkner's poetry only what escapes the mundane and the quotidian can be truly artistic. Throughout the 1920s Faulkner distinguished the significance of the material world from the fragile symbolic significance that the visionary artist attempted to achieve. The novel, he felt, was obliged to

2. James B. Meriwether, ed., "An Introduction for *The Sound and the Fury,*" *Southern Review,* N.S. 8 (Autumn 1972), 708–709.

deal primarily with "man in his sorry clay braving chance and circumstance," and so it was fundamentally hostile to visionary methods (*EPP* 101). "Material and aesthetic significance are not the same, but material importance can destroy artistic importance in spite of what we would like to believe."[3] Thus in the separate reviews of Joseph Hergesheimer's fiction and John Cowper Powys's *Ducdame* from which I have just been quoting, he argued that the overtly poetic and symbolic aspects of their prose had no place in a novel. Nevertheless, his own early novels depend upon precisely what he considered inappropriate in Hergesheimer and Powys. The first three novels (and also the unfinished draft of "Elmer") are not otherwise very like one another in style and theme, but each of them attempts to conform to a visionary conception of Art.

Faulkner's discovery that the novel can have its own kind of artistic significance amounts largely to a belated appropriation of the genre's most ordinary capacities. Indeed, for all that the new method took him several years to find and the rest of his creative life to develop fully, its essential premises are anything but arcane or complicated. Toward the end of his career Faulkner was able to say accurately of his own work that "you write a story to tell about people, man in his constant struggle with his own heart, the hearts of others, or with his environment" (*FU* 239). The statement, an enlargement upon his assertion in the Nobel Prize speech that a writer's subject ought to be the "human heart" in conflict," is an inoffensive enough platitude (*ESPL* 119). The speech has in fact been viewed with dismay by some critics as evidence of Faulkner's inability to understand the daring and complexity of his own best work. The sentiments are remarkable only in that the emphasis on story-

3. Carvel Collins, ed., "A Fourth Book Review by Faulkner," *Mississippi Quarterly*, 28 (Summer 1975), 353. The review originally appeared in the New Orleans *Times-Picayune* on March 22, 1925.

telling and on human conflict assumes the method he hadn't yet discovered in the early work.

In order for his materials to constitute a story, the novelist must ordinarily understand them to embody conflicts that do not instantly dissolve into harmony or stalemate. Likewise, according to literary standards that have not changed markedly since Homer, representing the story in a plot entails focusing the conflict by means of such narrative fundamentals as foreshortening, pacing, suspense, and climax. Faulkner's skillful management of such fundamentals has been demonstrated at length by Joseph Reed.[4] But although this skill is among the glories of Faulkner's mature prose, Reed's argument that Faulkner was first and foremost a storyteller does not hold for the early fiction. In fact, Faulkner's indifference to the need for dramatic conflict was the bane of his otherwise sympathetic editors at *Scribner's Magazine* in the 1920s.

> The trouble with your writing, it seems to me, is that you get mostly the overtones and seem to avoid the real core of the story. It would seem that in the attempt to avoid the obvious you have manufactured the vague. You are skirting around drama and not writing it. It might be worth while to attempt to tell a straightforward tale as you might narrate an incident to a friend, then all this atmosphere and all the background which you sketch in so skillfully will come right handy and make your work distinctive.[5]

The editor assumes, plausibly enough, that he and Faulkner are of one mind about the real core of a story. If they were, the decision to stress drama or to skirt it would be chiefly a question of selecting the locally more effective technique. But Faulkner is practicing an essentially different art in his early fiction, one that in Georg Lukács's terminology is

4. Joseph Reed, *Faulkner's Narrative* (New Haven 1973).
5. James B. Meriwether, ed., "Faulkner's Correspondence with *Scribner's Magazine,*" *Proof,* 3 (1972), 257.

descriptive rather than narrative.[6] As it happens, Lukács disapproved of Faulkner's writing, and he has cited *The Sound and the Fury* as an example of the antirealist modernism he deplored. Yet his distinction corresponds closely to the difference in Faulkner's work before and after 1929. It can help us to specify the important continuities between *The Sound and the Fury* and those nineteenth-century realistic novels that Faulkner has said that writing *The Sound and the Fury* first taught him how to read. Likewise, it can help us to isolate those aspects of the book and of Faulkner's earlier novels that belong to a symbolist art, against which Lukács's ideological objections may be more appropriate.

By the terms narration and description, Lukács refers less to specific literary techniques than to general modes of representation, each implying radically different ideas about the origins of textual meaning. Narrative art determines the meaning of specific elements in the text according to their relation to the concrete situation of the persons represented in the fictional world. "Objects come to life poetically only to the extent that they are related to men's lives; that is why the true epic poet does not describe objects but instead exposes their function in the mesh of human destinies."[7] This functional perspective gives depth and thickness to the fictional world, distributing elements into background or foreground according to their lesser or greater relevance to the represented human lives. Also, it allows that the meaning of objects and events can change as the human situation changes. The perspective is a consequence of narrative art's essential premise, that meaning is immanent in the world.

6. I draw primarily on "Narrate or Describe" in *Writers and Critics,* Arthur D. Kahn, trans. (New York 1971), 110–148, and *Realism in Our Time,* John and Necke Mander, trans. (New York 1971). These and several other relevant pieces may be found in volume 4 of Lukács's *Werke, Essays über den Realismus* (Neuwied and Berlin 1971).

7. "Narrate or Describe," 137. I have altered the translation slightly to make it conform to standard English usage.

The narrative artist's task is thus to discover and represent the meaning constituted by concrete human situations.

In descriptive art, however, the meaning of an object is no longer ultimately independent of the artistic description. The writer must impose significance on a world that has none of its own or at least none worth writing about. Hence the meaning of any element in the represented world must be measured by its relation to an external, necessarily abstract, and usually static concept. "The loss of the narrative interrelationship between objects and their function in concrete human experience means a loss of artistic significance. Objects can then acquire significance only through direct association with some abstract concept which the author considers essential to his view of the world. But an object does not thereby achieve poetic significance; significance is assigned to it. The object is made a symbol."[8] With respect to the fictional world, this concept is necessarily transcendental, and in visionary art it may well be so with respect to the writer's world also. In either case the concept warrants the meaning of the writer's text and governs his compositional techniques.

Lukács polemically draws the line between these two modes more sharply than can be fully justified. Without his occasionally naive epistemological self-confidence, one would have to say that the role played by the abstract concept in narration and in description differs more in degree than kind. Nevertheless, precisely the kind of symbolic description Lukács complains of is central in Faulkner's apprentice novels. Meaning in these works is largely conveyed by a play of verbal images that goes on independently of the situation of the characters. It is not that the objects represented in the world and described in often elaborate and highly poetic language cease to have any function in the characters' lives.

8. "Narrate or Describe," 131.

Rather, that function is plainly subordinate to the place of the object within the symbolic design of the text as a whole. Actions, objects, persons, and verbal images become fundamentally equivalent and interchangeable components, existing on a single plane and constituted with meaning by their relation to the writer's visionary concept. Foreground and background merge, for both take on meaning from their relation to a transcendental plane that is equally distant from either.

That Faulkner's early fiction belongs to Lukács's descriptive mode is not the result of a purely technical decision or a failure of skill. Faulkner fully intends his early novels to be like his poems in deriving their meaning primarily from a relation to a visionary absolute rather than from ordinary human situations. Joseph Blotner tells us that Balzac was one of the writers the young Faulkner most admired.[9] But Faulkner's sensibility was not initially so attuned to presenting the rough-hewn "truth about people" for which he later praised Balzac; instead his early fiction betrays more attention to "truth in a chalice," the concern for elegantly symbolic language and for the artful contrivance of images, surfaces, and details that he identifies in part with Flaubert (*FU* 55–56). Hence Faulkner tends to fashion his early fictional texts as single complex symbolic landscapes. Dialogue, plot, character, and milieu all become elements in a large, painterly still life.

Both of Faulkner's first two novels are motivated by a visionary concept, the realm of "splendid and timeless beauty" that Dawson Fairchild identifies in *Mosquitoes* as the province of the artist (*Mq* 339). By the last half of the 1920s Faulkner was already thinking of arrested motion as a metaphor for this transcendent realm and also for the work of art and the principle of artistic beauty. His most

9. Joseph Blotner, *Faulkner: A Biography* (New York 1977), I, 110, 160, 192.

eloquent statement of the effect of such art comes in *Mosquitoes,* when he describes the perception of a statue Gordon has sculpted.

> As you entered the room the thing drew your eyes: you turned sharply as to a sound, expecting movement. But it was marble, it could not move. And when you tore your eyes away and turned your back on it at last, you got again untarnished and high and clean that sense of swiftness, of space encompassed; but on looking again it was as before: motionless and passionately eternal—the virginal breastless torso of a girl, headless, armless, legless, in marble temporarily caught and hushed yet passionate still for escape, passionate and simple and eternal in the equivocal derisive darkness of the world. [*Mq* 11]

The statue bodies forth the passionate motion of its subject and yet preserves this meaningfulness as simple and eternal in the face of a world that encroaches on both characteristics. The sculptor's art is representational, at least in part and to begin with. But the arrest of the image in marble removes it from the world of which it begins as a representation. The removal, paradoxically preserving the world's motion and vitality, locates the statue in a realm of eternal essence. In other words, Gordon's statue is created under virtually the same aesthetic as Faulkner's poetry.

It is significant, however, that the most evocative example of this kind of art is found not in literature but in sculpture. None of the several writers gathered together in *Mosquitoes* is deemed a creator of genuine art in the way Gordon is, not even the poet Eva Wiseman, to whom Faulkner attributes several of his own most characteristic poems. The phrase, "arrested motion," in fact first appears in Faulkner's fiction to describe a statue (*NOS* 46). In the early part of his career sculpture and the plastic arts in general occupy the foremost place in Faulkner's conception of truly achieved art. The "Winged Victory" he had seen in

France in 1925 is one model he returns to several times; poem XVII of *A Green Bough,* for example, depicts the experience of viewing the statue.

As Faulkner seeks to move from lyric poetry to narrative fiction, however, the kind of art represented by sculpture offers less a usable model than a challenge and a series of aesthetic problems. He seems to search initially for a method that will allow him to reproduce the effects of spatial, plastic art in a medium with quite different properties and conventions. An extended narrative encompasses time quite as insistently as Gordon's marble encompasses space, for example. The single moment of transcendence isolated by the statue is only one part of the temporal expanse which the novelist is obliged to represent. And the conventions of fiction substitute for the relatively spare, formal relationships of texture, color, line, and shape the semantic complexities of human behavior in a teeming world.

Like Faulkner's poetry, sculpture is an art based on the free-standing image. The image, the holistic sum of the details of the poem or statue, is meant according to a symbolist aesthetic to carry the observer beyond its concrete referent and toward the transcendent realm. The image or symbol is itself both atomistic and static, a monadlike lens focused upon the purity of an ideal realm that cannot be glimpsed directly or unequivocally. To begin with at least, Faulkner conceives his task as the emulation in the novel of such an image-based art.

Faulkner's initial strategy in fiction is simply to locate the image in a temporal world. Keats's "Ode on a Grecian Urn," a poem that singularly commanded Faulkner's imagination throughout his career, offers the beginnings of a model for this. The urn, itself a plastic image of arrested motion, is translated into and virtually replaced by the poet's act of perception and meditation, an act that unfolds in time. Perceiving and meditating thus serve as rudimentary forms of human endeavor, and they open the way for representing more complex interactions of consciousness and environment.

One of the first pieces of fiction published by Faulkner, "New Orleans," employs a version of this strategy. The speakers of each of the eleven brief monologues rhapsodize on the things they desire or have desired in life. The point of the work as a whole is to express the universality of the human desire for beauty and splendor. However, the action in each sketch goes on entirely in the enclosed domain of the speaker's mind. In spite of the title, there is little sense of local environment in any of the monologues and virtually no interaction between the speaker and anything outside his mind. Nothing impinges but what is already an object of remembered or imagined desire.

The sketches are not static, but their dynamic quality arises almost entirely from the sequence of metaphors each speaker generates to describe his desideratum. In fact, the speaker and his situation in relation to the desired object are chiefly characterized by his struggle for expression and by the restless energy that drives him from one trope to another. Language, rather than other persons or a material environment, is the source of conflict in each sketch, for no single metaphor proves adequate to express the desire. "New Orleans" is an interesting piece of work, and its use of discontinuous expressions of desire for a central ideal anticipates one of the strategies of *The Sound and the Fury*. The possibility of significant action, however, is limited to the conflict between language and a partially ineffable ideal. This, after all, is no different from the method of the poetry.

The next important method Faulkner attempts is also strongly image-based, but it owes more to the notion of truth in a chalice than to Keats's ode. *Soldiers' Pay* practices an essentially decorative art. Although the book is not lacking in basic narrative effects, it bears the marks of an author whose affinities are with painting, sculpture, and lyric poetry. What signifies in the novel is not how people behave but how they look and what they are in essence. The initial belief in using imaginary scenes and people results in both being imagined as elements of a decorously composed picture plane. Even Margaret Powers, otherwise the novel's chief success in character portrayal, is explicitly and accurately likened to a figure in a Beardsley drawing. For all the mockery in his phrasing, Faulkner takes nearly the pains he attributes to Beardsley in always posing her "white and slim and depraved among meretricious trees and impossible marble fountains" (SP 31).

Januarius Jones is ostensibly one of the chief personages in the book, but his middle-aged, yellow-eyed, fat, and goatish figure is dressed out primarily for a formal contrast to the young, blinded, once athletic, and faunlike Donald Mahon. Jones hasn't much to do once he has been described other than act like a man who fits his description. Most of the relationships among the characters are primarily disclosed in this same way, through the contrast of poses and descriptions rather than through their actions. The relationships do not change or evolve so much as accumulate once the character has been introduced and has assumed his place in the static composition of the whole. It is as if each character were a figure in a tableau, whose full significance were constituted by his clothes, features, and posture and by his alignment with respect to similarly constituted figures in the composition.

The language of Soldiers' Pay is heavily metaphorical, often gaudily so, and the elaborately described scenery is as much an actor as any of the characters. At numerous points Faulkner quotes or silently echoes images from his own poems. Frequently, however, the language has very little to do with the human situation he presents. For instance, one image of leafy trees in May is a fine set piece, but it does little more for the narrative than mark the passage of time: "What were once tall candlesticks, silvery with white bloom, were now tall jade candlesticks of leaves beneath the blue cathedral of sky across which, in hushed processional, went clouds like choirboys, slow and surpliced" (*SP* 281). Not only does the ecclesiastic solemnity of this passage seem gratuitous with respect to the story, it even jars a bit with the otherwise consistently fecund and erotic quality of the nature imagery.

The importance of the imagery to Faulkner's conception of the novel is indicated by the frequency with which many of the images are repeated, often word for word. The images are asked to bear large burdens of signification, highlighting what the narrated action does not and thereby assuming the arbitrarily symbolic character Lukács condemns. Sometimes, as in the repeated references to the white-bellied tree in the rector's yard, this works quite well. But when Faulkner reaches for large, vague meanings about the sadness of life by describing Mahon's death as a "ship with twilight-colored sails dreaming on down the world," he doesn't help his cause by reaching three times in the space of four pages (*SP* 291, 292, 294). The image is that much more pretentious and unlikely if one recognizes that it originates in a poem about the Nativity, the one which became number XXIV in *A Green Bough*.

The most accurate criticism of *Soldiers' Pay,* which emphasizes both its picturesque charm and its narrative lifelessness, is the one prophetically administered by Faulkner in his 1922 review of Hergesheimer's work. Even though Faulkner is enough attracted by it that he will practice the same kind of "flawless prose" in a few years, he insists that such writing is not novelistic and that it risks exposing the author as an "emasculate priest surrounded by puppets he has carved and clothed and painted" (*EPP* 103).

Linda Condon, in which he reached his apex, is not a novel. It is more like a lovely Byzantine frieze: a few unforgettable figures in silent arrested motion, forever beyond the reach of time and troubling the heart like music. His people are never actuated from within; they do not create life about them; they are like puppets assuming graceful but meaningless postures in answer to the author's compulsions, and holding these attitudes until he arranges their limbs again in other gestures as graceful and as meaningless. [EPP 101–102]

Hergeshimer is genuinely concerned with visionary ideals in *Linda Condon*. However, by organizing his book as a kind of schematic *Bildungsroman,* the education of Linda into the three mysteries—love, spirit, and death—he is able to convey his neoplatonic vision with a far more adroit use of narrative than Faulkner manages in either of his first two novels.[10] If *Linda Condon* does culminate in something slightly resembling a Byzantine frieze, this pictorial stasis is a genuinely achieved vision, a moment that emerges directly out of the action of the story. *Soldiers' Pay* is to a far greater degree enclosed within and constrained by its tableaulike design from the outset.

In the Hergesheimer review, Faulkner has already begun to link a novel's significance with its ability to represent motion: Hergesheimer's is a "world without motion or meaning" (*EPP* 103). Nevertheless, Faulkner's method does not change significantly in his second novel. If *Mosquitoes* suffers from a few of the same difficulties as his first novel, however, it does so more bravely by making them explicit issues in the book. A fiction of ideas and social satire roughly in the tradition of Huxley, Peacock, and early Meredith, it gathers a group of representative bohemians together in a confined situation and lets them talk. A chief question they discuss is how the kind of art represented by Gordon's statue can be executed in what is otherwise the "utter and heartbreaking stupidity of words" (*Mq* 186).

The discussion of this question by the novelist Fairchild

10. Joseph Hergesheimer, *Linda Condon* (New York 1919).

and his friend Julius moves between two poles. One is a recognition of the "sterility" of language and a gentle, auto-biographically apt dismissal of the youthful poet's "childlike faith in the efficacy of words"; the other is an insistence that, brought together in "happy conjunction," words can not only produce vitality but even be "invested with some-thing not of this life, this world at all" (*Mq* 210, 249). The metaphors on the optimistic side continue to suggest that the goal is a holistic and quasi-magical arrangement of dis-crete elements which can evoke some distant and eternal beauty. What is crucial is that the elements be "brought together . . . in perfect proportions" (*Mq* 339). Then the text as a whole can become as effective a symbol as the statue. Like astrological bodies whose configurations govern life on a faraway earth, the elements of a narrative are asked to conjoin in order to signify the beauty of a timeless else-where. Although only Gordon's statue succeeds, the goal throughout the book is to achieve "splendid and timeless beauty," the ideal glimpsed in the visionary "instant of timeless beatitude" (*Mq* 339).

For all the advances it represents over the early fiction, *The Sound and the Fury* adheres to many of the goals and assumptions articulated in *Mosquitoes,* and there is reason to believe that the book began as an attempt to practice them unequivocally. Faulkner's numerous comments about the composition of *The Sound and the Fury* consistently empha-size the things in it that most resemble his earlier, image-based art. (To many of his readers and critics, Faulkner's convictions about the intentions and achievements of the novel have seemed curiously at odds with the actual text, but for the moment we are interested only in how the book can be seen to resemble his earlier work.) In virtually every statement Faulkner made in thirty years of speaking about the gestation of the novel, he insisted that it began with the luminous image of Caddy Compson and with the situation on the day of Damuddy's death. As Caddy was envisioned in the pastoral landscape at the branch and later peering in at the funeral, she became for Faulkner an image of the ideal beauty so often envisioned in the poetry. "To me she was the beautiful one, she was my heart's darling. That's what I wrote the book about . . . to try to tell, try to draw the picture of Caddy" (*FU* 6).

Notice that Faulkner abandons a narrative term, "tell," for a pictorial one. The goal remains the drawing of the static image. To the extent that his aim in *The Sound and the Fury* is primarily "to make myself a beautiful and tragic little girl," the book operates under the older method.[11] It seeks an ideal beauty through a single fixed and splendid image, Caddy Compson as a little girl on a particular day. As in the poetry, this ideal is to be seen only indirectly. We see her only through the eyes of her brothers. More important, we discover her significance not directly through the effects on them of her presence but indirectly and negatively through the suffering and intense longing occasioned by her absence.

Moreover, the conception of the scenes on the day of Damuddy's death suggests the pictorial method of *Soldiers' Pay*. At the branch and later outside the Compson house, the children are arranged in a tableau of postures and spatial relationships with Caddy at the center. Very little occurs in the novel to modify the tableau; we get the essential, unchanging meaning of each character in a scene occurring twenty years before most of the others in the novel. Jason's moral isolation and his self-defeating selfishness are visible in his posture, hands jammed in his pockets, and later when he trips over his own feet. Quentin's futile desire to protect and to dominate his sister appears in his reaction to her wetting her dress and in his constant lagging behind in

11. "An Introduction for *The Sound and the Fury*," 710.

resistance to her leadership. Benjy's dependence on Caddy is evident when she squats in the water before him to soothe and hush his fears. Lastly, Caddy's tenderness is represented by the affectionate attention to Benjy, and her boldness by the insistence on climbing the tree to view the funeral.

The tableau is partly duplicated on a completely different level by the structural relationships of the novel's first three sections. Carried to completion, the duplication would contribute to a singularly static and self-enclosed method. Even as we moved through the three sections, we would proceed as though from one vantage point to another on a grouped configuration of statues, only to find that our steps have traced that very configuration. From each of the vantage points, so Faulkner insists, the intent is to give us an increasingly clearer view of Caddy and the ideal she represents.

In fact, Caddy becomes less important in each successive part of the novel. But her decreasing centrality does not necessarily compromise the centrality of the ideal. Even in Benjy's section, Caddy's significance is manifested most forcefully in the intense pain he feels at her absence. The other three sections are equally devoted to showing the pain caused by loss and absence, including but not limited to the absence of Caddy. The closely parallel emotional patterns in the novel's four sections are emphasized in a striking essay by Carey Wall.[12] Wall insists on the importance of states of feeling and sequences of emotion even at the expense of their causes and the concrete circumstances surrounding them. Her essay is implicitly directly against more orthodox readings of the novel, which find in it situations, issues, and events that need to be explained. A novel which truly adhered to the old method and focused on creating emotional intensities would, like a Swinburne

12. Carey Wall, *"The Sound and the Fury:* The Emotional Center," *Midwest Quarterly,* 11 (Summer 1970), 371–387.

poem, be singularly resistant to such an explication of content. Details and circumstances would not matter much; the particularities of each brother's situation and the objective conditions of the world the Compsons live in would fade before the common intensity of their suffering and the absent radiance at the center of each monologue. Quentin's anguished debate with his father over the meaning of life would be only an extended sign for the same thing expressed by the battered slipper and the smells of honeysuckle, gasoline, and camphor.

We would thus have a visionary novel based on images of absence, tableaulike configurations, and patterns of emotion, all signifying a pure, fleeting essence of beauty and wholeness.

This is not what most readers and critics have found in *The Sound and the Fury*, a book that after all seems to have something intelligible to say about the world. Yet the novel's obvious themes—the decay of the Old South, the human response to time and change, the relation of childhood experience to adult behavior—are no more exclusively the business of the book than the evocation of a visionary ideal is. Such themes are among the ones expressed by the new method, which seems virtually to be born within the pages of the novel. But although *The Sound and the Fury* inaugurates the new method, it does not embrace it fully or even with the tenacity of the stories and novels that follow shortly afterward.

The seeds of the new method can be noticed in the closing pages of *Mosquitoes*. Fairchild's final pronouncement on the question of art introduces a newly temporal aspect to the speculations. He celebrates the still-to-be-desired "instant of timeless beatitude" but places it in mute, unexplained, apposition to "the Passion Week of the heart" (*Mq* 339). With the advantage of hindsight we can observe here the first small step toward a new idea of the artistically meaningful.

It is made possible by Fairchild's connecting two kinds of time, the momentary instant of timeless beatitude in which visionary ideals may be glimpsed and the historical duration of a Passion Week, whose significance derives also from the dramatic conflict occurring within it. The almost casual linking Fairchild makes is a slender enough clue, but it offers the first possibility of understanding temporal existence to be as meaningful as eternal essence. The link is made firm by Faulkner's new use of arrested motion. Occasionally in *Sartoris/Flags in the Dust,* and more assiduously in *The Sound and the Fury,* Faulkner focuses on the process of seeking the visionary realm. As he does, arrested motion comes to represent more than the fundamental artistic vision and the goal of all true works of art. Faulkner begins to attend to the activity, the process of arresting motion, as well as the result. Arresting motion emerges as an object of representation potentially as significant for art as arrested motion, the otherworldly essence sought by the poet or the faun.

Like the yearning for beauty and splendor in "New Orleans," this activity occurs in the everyday world. Indeed, a character's wanting to arrest motion henceforth becomes the principal metaphor for all such yearnings. Therefore when Horace Benbow or one of the Compson brothers tries to halt the motion of life, the attempt is both meaningful in itself and an instance of a universally significant activity. Arresting motion becomes an immanently meaningful action. In *Soldiers' Pay* Faulkner had had something to describe, "the longing of mankind for a Oneness with Something, somewhere," and he portrayed it in a static, pictorial composition (*SP* 319). Beginning primarily in *The Sound and the Fury,* he has something to narrate, the attempts of the characters to arrest motion, envisioned as a dynamic interaction between an arresting consciousness and a fluid, phenomenal environment.

The fundamental step here is toward objectifying and externalizing the subjective practices of the poetry. Faulkner's poetic quest for timeless beauty and significance becomes the characteristic action of the people in his fiction. At first the action is meaningful only in terms of the goal that will make it unnecessary; the quest for eternal essence is significant because the ideal is not immediately present in the world. Increasingly, however, arresting motion is meaningful on its own. This opens the way for a reversal of the poetry's manner of generating meaning. The pure quest for the ideal is modulated by attention to the quest as an event with important implications in and for the temporal world. The visionary ideal begins to be displaced by the envisioning of it and the symbol by the symbolizing. The four successive parts of *The Sound and the Fury* can, in fact, be read as stages in just such a displacement. The crucial issue is the status of the ideal. Once the search for it becomes significant in itself and the world of time is granted its own priority, Faulkner's art need no longer depend so utterly on a vision of transcendence. Thus what begins by validating the temporal world as a kind of staging area from which the ideal is sought may end by testing the desire for the ideal against its effects on temporal existence.

Few such doubts about the necessity of an ideal realm are manifest in Benjy's section, which in isolation is the one most governed by the older method. The single image and the timeless ideal are still the centers for the section in which, Faulkner assures us, "the story is all there."[13] Faulkner recognizes fully that Benjy is "like something eyeless and voiceless which might have lived, existed merely

13. James B. Meriwether, ed., "An Introduction to *The Sound and the Fury*," *Mississippi Quarterly*, 26 (Summer 1973), 414. This is another, presumably earlier, version of the preface published in the *Southern Review*.

because of its ability to suffer."[14] This is exactly why he is so useful as a center of consciousness; his suffering is an unequivocal index of the absence of the ideal. At least to begin with, Benjy is not the moral touchstone that some critics have seen him as; his demands upon the world are as absolute and impossible as those of his brothers. Instead, Benjy is a touchstone for identifying an ideal world and a means of demonstrating its overriding importance. For Benjy the image of Caddy, that of a world of beauty and plenitude, is a purely external thing which is either given or withheld. Because he has never matured from the time at which she meant so much to him, both the full radiance of her presence and the intense agony of her absence continue to be maintained as the simple, timeless conditions of a wholly objective world.

In other words, because Benjy is so much the passive register of events, very little intervenes to divert us from the atemporal image of Caddy around which his world organizes itself. To a far greater degree than in the later sections, the stream of consciousness in Benjy's section is instrumental, a means for the expression of the ideal, rather than an intrinsically significant activity of the mind. The focus is not displaced toward the perceiving and imagining and shaping activities that dominate Quentin's and Jason's inner lives. The significance of the nonchronological storytelling in this part does not lie solely in the wish to represent the mental life of an idiot plausibly. It lies also in the principled refusal to temporalize the expression of what is fundamentally and radically atemporal, the vision that Caddy represents to Benjy.

Benjy's status as a passive register is by no means unqualified, however. The seeds of a displacement already exist in his narrative, and they are brought into sharper relief

14. "An Introduction to *The Sound and the Fury*," 414.

by the way later sections encourage us to reinterpret the first one. Benjy is fully capable of recognizing absence, though not the change which brought it about, and to a limited extent he works to alleviate the pain of absence. Just as he moves in the company of his nurses to the gate, the swing, and the pasture—scenes of remembered presence—so his mind continually returns to the day of his renaming and the day of Damuddy's death. If the movement of his consciousness is no willed escape into a more comforting past, because Benjy hardly distinguishes between past and present and only barely possesses a conscious will, it is at least an instinctive leaning toward pleasant sensations.

In Quentin's section the significance of the narrator's attempt to shape his world is more pronounced. The one-dimensional contrast between presence and absence in Benjy's section is replaced by a more complex conflict between the actualities of the world and the ideals Quentin demands of it. The ideal is not represented for Quentin in given, objective images; rather it is something he is struggling to find or create or reestablish images of. Thus his quest serves as a way of expressing a complaint about the world he lives in. Quentin insists on the radical distinction between eternal essence and temporal existence which is assumed in the poetry. Like the speakers of many of the poems, he demands that things have significance exclusively in terms of the eternal. As Quentin, his father, and almost all critics of the novel agree, Quentin's enemy is time. Because he is so deeply aware of this, his narrative demands a privileged position in the novel. He articulates the frustration about time and change and decay which his brothers can only experience.

Nothing can be meaningful for him if it is not permanent and absolute. "If people could only change one another forever that way merge like a flame swirling up for an instant then blown cleanly out along the cool eternal dark"

(*SF* 219). But Quentin recognizes all too well that everything he sees and does is impermanent, ambiguous, and
temporal. He understands to his sorrow that ideals find no
objective confirmation in the world; they are only ideals.
The material world therefore becomes a storehouse of images which mock his desire for the ideal. Every reflection of
the world—including his own shadow, all black persons,
and even the memories of his own attempts to implement
his ideals—conspires to mock him. In the poems, twilight is
often the time when the visionary realm is most discernable,
and to Quentin also it offers a "quality of light as if time
really had stopped for a while" (*SF* 209–210). But twilight
is actually the worst time of all for him, because it commin-
gles the ideal and the actual so grotesquely, demanding recognition of their incompatibility. "Down a long corridor of
grey halflight where all stable things had become shadowy
paradoxical all I had done shadows all I had felt suffered
taking visible form antic and perverse mocking without
relevance inherent themselves with the denial of the significance they should have affirmed" (*SF* 211).

Quentin's complaint about the world is itself an indication of displacement. By shifting attention away from the
timeless ideal, the novel moves toward taking the temporal
world seriously as artistic material. More importantly, the
dramatization of the quest serves to particularize and temporalize the ideal realm, to present it as a phenomenon of the
imperfect world of everyday life. However much Quentin's
ideals are pure and universal, we are shown that they also
proceed directly from his personal, worldly idiosyncracies.
This serves to diminish the claim made by Quentin (and by
Faulkner in the poetry) about their significance. Quentin
wants to see himself as a knight of the ideal, challenging or
spurning the temporal world in the name of pure ideals. But
the particularity of his situation compromises the purity of
the quest. His ideals spring from an intensely personal situa-

tion, as does his failure to attain them. Although virginity is a traditional enough symbol of uncorrupted essence, the excessive importance Quentin attaches to it is clearly also the result of his neurotic dread of sexuality. "It seemed to me that I could hear whispers secret surges smell the beating of hot blood under wild unsecret flesh watching against red eyelids the swine untethered in pairs rushing coupled into the sea" (*SF* 219). Likewise, the loss of Caddy is not simply a sign of lost beauty and wholeness, as it is for Benjy. It is also an image of Quentin's personal inability to control his world, either physically by making his sister obey or metaphysically by dictating what the significance of her behavior will be. She is as much the opponent in his struggle to demand timeless significance as she is the object of the struggle. He is still trying to say to her and to the world, "Im stronger than you" (*SF* 191).

Quentin wants to believe himself a "man of courage" who is faithful enough to his ideals to be willing to die for them (*SF* 219). His watery grave will then be the longed-for world of purity, another version of the exclusive hell with its *"clean flame the two of us more than dead"* (*SF* 144). As is true of death in many of the poems, the death Quentin imagines for himself will be the attainment of a region where things truly "finished themselves" (*SF* 97). Even Christ on Judgment Day will be unable to command him to rise, so utter and absolute will be his drowning. Yet for all these heroic posturings, Quentin is obsessed by and unable to refute his father's contention that the only thing that could drive his son to suicide would be a recognition of weakness and failure. "No you will not do that until you come to believe that even she was not quite worth despair" (*SF* 221). Only out of a fear that he is not strong enough to maintain his private symbols of the ideal permanently will he resort to suicide—so, just before he leaves to do the deed, Quentin hears his father predicting.

The question in all this is how we are to take Quentin's vision of the ideal and his failure either to attain it or to find some way of living without it. Quentin's plight is in some ways universal but in all ways personal. On the one hand, his complaint about the world is surely offered as something to be taken quite seriously, and its accuracy is confirmed by the rest of the novel. This is precisely what Mark Spilka recognizes in an essay in which he struggles manfully to rescue Quentin's narrative from the genre of case history.[15] But at the same time Quentin's failure to attain the ideal and even his need to do so are depicted as uniquely and neurotically his own. The effect is to temporalize the ideal, to blur the radical distinction between the eternal and the temporal by showing that the desire for timeless essence is governed by particularity and temporality.

We are thus not quite allowed to see Quentin as a representative protagonist in the human quest for beauty and significance. This is of course how the speakers of the poems ask to be seen, but the objectification and ironic distancing accomplished in Quentin's section supplies an implicit critique of these poems as deluded and sentimental. What does seem representative about Quentin's plight is the genuine intensity of the pain he suffers. His intellect and his sensitivity thus function as equivalent to Benjy's idiocy; they establish a further register of the pain of loss and absence.

By the time we reach Jason's section the displacement may appear almost complete. The concentration on the narrator's activity, his attempt to control his world by word and deed, seems undiluted by a vision of an ideal realm where such arduous struggles are unnecessary. Jason does not even seem to share the kind of anguish which dominates his brothers' monologues; certainly the loss of Caddy does not loom for him as it does for them. He believes that he

15. Mark Spilka, "Quentin Compson's Universal Grief," *Contemporary Literature*, 11 (Autumn 1970), 451–469.

has been shrewd enough to cut his losses and even to be receiving compensation for them. His financial chicanery, particularly the embezzlement of his niece's money, and the pleasures of cruelty to such as Caddy and Luster are nearly equitable recompense for the purely secular losses he will admit to. The acceptance of such compensation, so Jason (and Faulkner by ironically pronouncing him sane in the "Compson Appendix") argues, is evidence of his superiority to the self-defeating Compson sentimentality.

Much of the horror and also the satiric force of the portrayal of Jason derives from the pettiness of his confessed emblem of loss, the job at Herbert Head's bank, in comparison to his brothers' symbols. No pure ideal seems to attach to Jason's desires or to be signified by his evident pain and frustration. Yet the deeper horror of Jason's situation is the extent to which loss of the job substitutes for a more intense and emotional loss. It is not simply that Jason's desires make his brothers' look noble in contrast; it is that his desires have been twisted so as to deny the emotional needs all three have in common. For Jason also indicates, despite himself, that an earlier, repressed source of his pain is the absence of love and stability in the family. As with Benjy and Quentin, the positive ideal is located in childhood, but for Jason it is not Caddy who is the center but his father and namesake.

Twice Mrs. Compson reproaches Jason for speaking bitterly of his father. Yet Jason's scorn, like Quentin's horror over Caddy's loss of honor, is rooted in a feeling that an ideal has failed him. The almost hysterical concern for his own current position as a quasi-father in the household and the half-admitted sorrow he expresses at Mr. Compson's funeral suggest that behind this scorn is a disappointed image of the father as an anchor of meaningfulness in a healthy family. Most of Jason's numerous references to his father reflect the bitterness; all of them presuppose the importance to him of the ideal father who is not alcoholic, who does not let the fortune and status of his family decline, and who does not love Caddy and Quentin more than Jason.

Jason's sorrow for the loss of this ideal father, the father he wanted or expected or once believed Mr. Compson to be, is obliquely revealed at Mr. Compson's funeral. "We stood there, looking at the grave, and then I got to thinking about when we were little and one thing and another and I got to feeling funny again, kind of mad or something" (*SF* 252). Jason is embarrassed and uncomfortable about the sentiment, admitting it only by saying several times that he feels "funny." He overcomes the emotion only by performing an otherwise gratuitous act of cruelty, swindling Caddy about seeing her child. The horror of this act, at first glance about the nearest thing to motiveless malignity we see in Jason, reveals both the intensity of his feeling and the way he typically deals with such emotions: transferring them to the loss of the bank job, punishing someone for this loss, and seeking financial compensation for it. "And so I counted the money again that night and put it away, and I didn't feel so bad. I says I reckon that'll show you. I reckon you'll know now that you cant beat me out of a job and get away with it" (*SF* 255). He congratulates himself that he has advanced beyond the trusting sentimentality of his youth. "I was a kid then. I believed folks when they said they'd do things. I've learned better since" (*SF* 256).

Jason's narrative is a record of his attempt to control a world he can no longer trust. His unflagging and almost completely unsuccessful struggle is to establish by strength of will a fixed order of behavior in the household. Once the fixity is assured he will at last be able to rest in "peace and quiet" in the place of the esteemed father (*SF* 257). Hence his anxiety over the town's opinion of his family and his frantic (and from the reader's perspective, deeply ironic) insistence to his mother about observing the forms of family decorum: "As long as I am buying food for people younger than I am, they'll have to come to the table to eat it. . . . I cant have all this whoop-de-do and sulking at mealtimes. I know that's a lot to ask her, but I'm that way in my own house. Your house, I meant to say" (*SF* 320–321).

Jason's self-presentation unwittingly accomplishes a satiric exposure of his belief that he can and does control his world by force of will and by a pragmatic readiness to accept compensation for his daily reverses. Jason's beliefs are as self-defeating as their opposite, the passivity and absolutism that both Benjy and Quentin display. In the "Appendix," it is almost as if Faulkner had taken pity on Jason and granted him his paltry success. He is allowed to live a "domestic, uxurious, connubial" weekend life with his Memphis whore, a situation in which familial stability is assured by the good money Jason pays for it (*SF* 422).

The first three sections of *The Sound and the Fury* form an obvious unit unto themselves, each a transcription of the mind of one of the Compson brothers living in the temporal world and seeking in some way to attain a time- less one. The prestige of the timeless ideal declines con- tinuously throughout the first three sections, until little re- mains in Jason's of the pure, noble plenitude experienced by Benjy and demanded by Quentin. For each brother the ideal is a projection from childhood; for each it derives from a need, increasingly portrayed as sentimental, neu- rotic, or self-deceiving, to reconstitute an image of the past. But even after the displacement of the desired ideal from Benjy's objective and radiant world of presence, the distinction between the two realms, the timeless and the temporal, continues to be posited. The timeless is increas- ingly implicated in the temporal as an extension or projec- tion of personal needs, but to the consciousness of each brother, it remains distinct, a world which is other than and elsewhere from what exists.

The final section of the novel, written in the third person, marks the final displacement of the ideal and the most undiluted commitment of the novel to the world of existence. Consciousness as such recedes from view, and we witness for the first time the materiality of the world. The shift is heralded in the opening image of the section, where the weather is shown "precipitating" a "substance" like "minute and venomous particles" on Dilsey's flesh (*SF* 330). The passage depicts the impingement of hostile forces on the self, and this, of course, is essentially what all three previous sections had portrayed. Now, however, the radical distinction between the interiority of the self and the exteriority of the world disappears. To Quentin the emanations of the self—shadows, reflections, and memories—had threatened to become part of the alien substance of the temporal world which mocked the ideals so carefully guarded in the mind. Now self and world are not alien to each other; both are seen principally as substance behaving in time.

Substance is portrayed as lasting and yet bearing prominently the marks of time, like the "patina, as though from the soles of bare feet in generations," of the earth around Dilsey's cabin door (*SF* 331). Dilsey herself is so much fleshy substance scarred by time and yet enduring within it, "as though muscle and tissue had been courage or fortitude which the days or the years had consumed until only the indomitable skeleton was left rising like a ruin or a landmark above the somnolent and impervious guts" (*SF* 331). Later we see the tears slide down her pitted cheeks "in and out of the myriad corruscations of immolation and abnegation and time" (*SF* 368). Her eroded substance participates in the action which is the last section's exclusive focus, the struggle to cope with the temporal weathering to which all is subject. For the marks of time on her flesh are not simply scars representing time's inevitable victories, but corruscations, points of incandescence that represent resistance to the erosion.

The action narrated in the first three sections is primarily mental, the action of consciousness in the world. But consciousness in the last section is no longer something apart. It is no longer private and remote, no longer capable of hoarding a precious image of the ideal and devoted to this task. The narrator reports the contents of Jason's mind no differently than the contents of niece Quentin's bedroom. All is part of temporal existence, and all signifies something important about the concrete situation of human life in a particular time and place. Temporal existence emerges as fully meaningful in itself and not merely a means of passage or a mocking contrast to the pure ideals of consciousness.

The timeless ideal is incorporated into the last section in the promise of Christian salvation implicit in Reverend Shegog's sermon. One may without too great violence to the text read the last section as an endorsement of Christian ideals. Such a reading would assimilate the novel to the celebration of less peculiarly religious ideals which Faulkner's poems and his earlier novels accomplish by somewhat different means. According to such a reading, the Passion Week of the heart would derive its meaning wholly from the transcendent realm for which it is a worldly preparation. Correspondingly, one would find in Faulkner's art another of the many aesthetic programs based on a theory of incarnation, the Logos of Christ serving as the exemplary bridge between time and eternity.

Yet for an Easter sermon Reverend Shegog's is curiously lacking in emphasis on the Resurrection. He dwells instead on suffering in the temporal world and on the generations passing away. The refrain of his sermon is "I got the recollection and the blood of the Lamb." In other words, I maintain in the awareness of my own suffering and in my own ravaged bodily substance a share in the pains of Jesus's life on earth. Dilsey and the rest of the congregation are asked to share the memory of the worldly pains of Jesus and Mary and to do so almost without reference to the eternal realm promised to those who remember and believe. Rather than depending primarily on a transcendental, theological sanction for its obviously beneficial effects, the service celebrates a worldly existence that gains its deepest significance and becomes most bearable when it is recognized as part of a collective suffering with a long and honorable past. Such recognition is what the episode explicitly dramatizes when the individual members of the congregation join together in the service and when they come to include in their midst the memory of all the previous generations.

This is not to say that the specific religious context of the sermon has no importance, only that the issue is not Christianity as such nor even a less doctrinal vision of an eternal realm. It is often asserted that Dilsey, unlike the Compson brothers, sees the present as part of a continuum that includes both time and eternity. "I seed de beginnin, en now I sees de endin" (*SF* 371). This seems true enough, although the ending she sees here is apparently the end of the Compson household and not a vision of glory. But the specific nature of her beliefs is not that essential; certainly Faulkner supplies only the most sketchy details. What is important is that the beliefs are measured by her behavior in the temporal world. True or false, inspired or illusory, the ideals celebrated in the service provide an "annealment" of Dilsey's ravaged substance (*SF* 371). Her indomitable skeleton is enabled to go on resisting consumption. What signifies about Dilsey is the way she behaves in trying to preserve the family, her actions in resistance to the consuming power of time. Belief in Christianity is one of her means of accepting and dealing with the world, and the belief is applauded precisely to the extent it enables her to do so.

To weigh the ideal for its effect on the temporal directly reverses Faulkner's initial method, which was to represent the temporal as a means of demonstrating the necessity of the ideal. Dilsey, who emerges as a substitute for Caddy at the center of the household and a displacement of her, is a concrete representation of the meaningfulness of temporal existence rather than a poetic symbol of the absolute. Dilsey's actions are meaningful as a way of living in time, not as a strategy for escaping it. To conceive Dilsey's life as fit material for art is to forgo the visionary quest for splendid and timeless beauty, or rather to redefine utterly what is meant by such beauty. The Passion Week of the heart, a struggling in time to cope with time, reveals itself as suitable material for the artist. Faulkner's method then becomes very much the traditional art of the novel, a narration of day-to-day existence in which are to be found immanently significant human conflicts.

The method of the last section is not, of course, the method of *The Sound and the Fury* as a whole. The intensity of the yearning for the ideal in the earlier sections is hardly abolished by Dilsey's resolute struggle with the here and the now or by Faulkner's belated discovery of the intrinsic meaningfulness of the human experience of time. We would certainly be perverse in reading Benjy's section as an exposure of a lamentably false consciousness. Dilsey's Christianity does nothing to refute Quentin's vision of a Christ "that not for me died not" (*SF* 218). "The grave hopeless sound of all voiceless misery under the sun" is still voiced by Benjy at the end, and it can be soothed only by the mechanical arrangement of "each in its ordered place" (*SF* 395, 401).

Nevertheless, although the yearning for transcendence remains a powerful motive *in* the novel, one too poignantly rendered to be simply a pretext for ironic deflation, it is gradually abandoned as the motive *of* the novel. Objects and characters and events cease to be described (as they so often are in the earlier fiction) as symbols of an otherworldly realm or of the longing to attain it. Instead they are presented according to a version of the narrative method made traditional in the nineteenth century as elements whose function in the text and whose significance in the fictional world are determined by the human experience of time. The static image sought for in the composition of the earlier work gets replaced by a representation of process and motion. The result in *The Sound and the Fury* is a work poised between the visionary and the realistic. But the very juxtaposition of the two is on the side of the new method as Faulkner now conceives it, for it is a means of objectifying and dramatizing the conflict between them.

4

The Referential Phase

Although *The Sound and the Fury* inaugurates the second major phase in Faulkner's career, it is not the most useful example of the mode that characterizes his writings in the early 1930s. *As I Lay Dying* is the exemplary text. That term requires definition, however, for I use it in a somewhat restricted way. Likewise in need of definition are the phases themselves or, rather, the criteria by which boundaries may be drawn between what will be variously called the phases, episodes, or moments in the career.

As I Lay Dying is exemplary first because it manifests a number of important themes and techniques which can also be found in the other novels published between 1929 and 1932: *The Sound and the Fury, Sanctuary,* and *Light In August.* More important, *As I Lay Dying* most fully manifests the enabling principles of all these texts. Most important of all, because it follows out these principles so unequivocally, it begins to reveal the limitations and contradictions in them which subsequently impel the writer to go beyond such principles. A text is exemplary, then, not so much because it is typical of all the others, but because it exhibits the most thorough development of the tendencies they have in common and is the one that reveals the problems on which the next phase of the career is based.

Texts thus belong to a single phase because they share

many of the same enabling principles. This, however, is decidedly and necessarily an inexact standard of definition. To divide any developing system into periods is always a somewhat arbitrary act, especially at the border between one state or period and another. Faulkner's career is no exception. By grouping several texts into one phase, I do not mean to imply that what they have in common so outweighs their differences as to link them inescapably to one another or to differentiate them radically from all of Faulkner's other writings. The differences between phases should, I hope, be clear, and so should the developmental relation. But the chronological and bibliographical boundaries between one phase and the next are necessarily provisional and also relatively inconsequential.

The rather sharp differences in Faulkner's writings before and after *The Sound and the Fury* are thus the exception. This transition period is the only one Faulkner seems to have consciously experienced as a breakthrough rather than an orderly development. Such a major transformation is by no means unique to Faulkner. A number of other writers whose roots are in romanticism have undergone much the same kind of change in style and method. The difference between Faulkner's first and second phases is, for example, analogous to the difference Robert Browning understood between subjective and objective poetry.[1] Like Browning forgoing the Shelleyan mode of *Pauline* and *Paracelsus* for the objectivity of the dramatic monologue, Faulkner moves from a highly subjective lyricism to the newly impersonal fiction of the early 1930s. Displacing the visionary quest for the absolute onto his characters allows Faulkner to set his poetic themes and images at a distance and to open them to a more ironic treatment.

A more appropriate parallel for Faulkner's new stance to-

1. Cf. Robert Browning, "Essay on Shelley," *Poetry and Prose,* Simon Nowell-Smith, ed. (Cambridge, Mass. 1951), 671–686.

ward his art is the posture of Stephen Dedalus's God, the aloof and disembodied creator contemplating his work from a plane above or beyond or behind it. The comparison is more fitting because Faulkner was surely influenced more directly by Joyce and other modern exponents of artistic impersonality than by Browning. He seems to have been well aware that impersonality was a prominent slogan of the modernist movement. As early as 1921, two years after T. S. Eliot had published "Tradition and the Individual Talent," Faulkner used the word as a casual token of praise in reviewing a volume of Conrad Aiken's poetry (*EPP* 75). The influence of the modernists' argument for impersonality on Faulkner's new conception of the novel in the years immediately after 1928 seems, in fact, to have been the last major external literary influence on his career. After this time the internal discipline of the career is far the more important source of changes in his literary practices.

For T. E. Hulme, Eliot, and Joyce's Stephen, the most influential English-speaking advocates of the concept, impersonality is a means of avoiding the emotional and rhetorical excesses of nineteenth-century English romantic verse. For Eliot in particular, it is a way of treating essentially romantic themes without falling prey to what is feared as the naive and mawkish clamor of direct lyric utterance. Faulkner seems to follow their reasoning. In fact, his path from the subjective and visionary art of *The Marble Faun* to the more objective, hard-edged art of *As I Lay Dying* places him more squarely within the modernistic movement than any other American novelist. The same path can be traced in the careers of Joyce, Eliot, Pound, Yeats, Stevens, and Williams. Between the course of Yeats, who achieved considerable success in an essentially nineteenth-century mode before making himself over in mid-career, and that of William Carlos Williams, who quickly abandoned the Keatsian voice of his first volume, the *Poems* of 1909, can be found the paradigmatic career

of the modernist poet. The modernist writer defines his objectivity in reaction to the nineteenth-century romantic verse
he had himself begun by practicing. Faulkner, along with
Joyce, became this sort of modernist only in his fiction.

When Faulkner explains the value of impersonality to a
reporter in 1931, however, he does not speak of a display of
the author's personality or a direct expression of his vision
as wickedly romantic. He says only that such display gets in
the way of the story.

> Mr. Faulkner had a very interesting idea, centering about the
> thesis that Dostoevski could have written the *Brothers* in one
> third the space had he let the characters tell their own stories
> instead of filling page after page with exposition. In the future
> novel, or fiction—Mr. Faulkner contends—there will be no
> straight exposition, but instead, objective presentation, by
> means of soliloquies or speeches of the characters, those of each
> character printed in a different colored ink. Something of the
> play technique will thus eliminate much of the author from the
> story. And the consequent loss of personality? Is not all writing
> interesting and important only insofar as it expresses the per-
> sonality of the author? All exclusive of the story, Mr. Faulkner
> says, is dead weight. [LG 18][2]

The manner of presentation is not here an important issue in
itself, as it generally was for the poets. The story, conceived
as an independent entity that belongs as much to the characters as the writer, is the primary value.[3] An objective,

2. Several of Faulkner's comments to the reporter from the University of Virginia student weekly seem to be in jest, and the remark about
The Brothers Karamazov may well be among these. But the idea of print-
ing speeches in different colored ink, for example, Faulkner took very
seriously indeed at the time. Cf. *Selected Letters,* 44–45, 71, 74.

3. Faulkner habitually speaks of "story" as an independent entity
which is shaped in order to produce the piece of fiction. He seems to mean
by the term what the Russian Formalists called the *fabula,* the chronological
or causal sequence of events, as opposed to the *sujet,* the presentation of
events in a text. I have followed Faulkner's usage throughout, although
criticism in English (following E. M. Forster) usually means something
like a *sujet* by "story," reserving the term "plot" for the other entity.

impersonal technique is to be preferred because it is the most efficient way of telling the story. (Such a theory says nothing about the origins of the story, which may be as deeply personal as in Eliot's *Waste Land* or, one assumes, Faulkner's *Sound and the Fury*.)

An impersonal technique, then, is for Faulkner preeminently instrumental. It is a device in the service of the story rather than a thing of independent value. Such an attitude toward technique is one hallmark of referential art. The thing represented takes clear priority over the means of representation. Literary form aspires to become a transparent medium of expression. We can see a few consequences of this attitude in *Light in August*. The book makes more extensive use of the conventions of Victorian realism, themselves essentially referential, than any other of Faulkner's major works.[4] But *Light in August* violates several of the potent formal norms of that otherwise generous tradition. Faulkner is more than usually willing in the book to sacrifice the established proprieties of the well-made novel to local exigencies of the material. For example, he is content to leave the stories of the three protagonists, Joe Christmas, Lena Grove, and Wayne Hightower, only loosely integrated. More strikingly, he defies proportion and tidiness by introducing late in the novel and without preparation several important new characters (Percy Grimm, Gavin Stevens, and the furniture salesman) and a radically new thematic personification (the Player who directs men's actions).

Broadly speaking, all of Faulkner's mature fiction is realistic and representational in intention. It refers to a real world that is posited to exist independently of the text, and it is intended to re-present that world. But the directly ref-

4. Michael Millgate points out the affinity with Hardy and Dickens and also reflects on the "apparent crudity" of the technique in *The Achievement of William Faulkner* (New York 1971), 124–137.

erential impulse is strongest in the novels published between 1929 and 1932. By referential I mean a representational art in which the act of representation does not itself come explicitly into question. Such an art may, like Faulkner's, be formally adventurous and even experimental, but the experiment is conducted only for the sake of the results it promises: as direct and accurate a presentation of the story as possible. The novels of Faulkner's referential phase otherwise differ from one another considerably, but all of them strive to make form and technique into transparent instruments of expression. All of them subordinate to the immediate representation of the world's motion the self-reflexive concerns prominent in Faulkner's writings before and after. In particular they pay little attention to the things that become crucial later on, the shaping and forming activities of the writer or the relation of his work to the culture at large.

A more obvious hallmark of referential art is its commitment to the primacy of concrete, worldly experience. We have seen how this emerges in *The Sound and the Fury*. The most important thematic implication of the commitment is the increased centrality of motion and the somewhat altered understanding of it. Worldly existence, when it was attended to at all in the writings of the visionary phase, was also usually characterized by motion, but this was then understood primarily as mutability, decay, and the pointless bustle of human endeavor. In the 1930s motion is understood more neutrally as the omnipresence of time and change. The representation of such motion is the chief goal of Faulkner's referential art. More specifically, the referential novels seek to portray motion in, through, and as the actions of the characters who attempt to cope with it. Adams has pointed out one of Faulkner's principal techniques for dramatizing a universal flux.[5] Like doomed and

5. Richard P. Adams, *Faulkner: Myth and Motion* (Princeton 1968), 6–14.

stubborn swimmers in a flooded river, Quentin Compson, Horace Benbow, and Darl Bundren (among others) all move athwart the prevailing flow, revealing its force by their resistance to it.

Motion is experienced most intensely in *The Sound and the Fury* and *Sanctuary* as the erosion of a supposedly static, innocent world. In both novels the static world is associated with childhood, and in both it is destroyed by sexuality. Horace Benbow looks at a still photograph of his beloved niece and suffers a hallucinated vision of Temple Drake's corruption imposed on it. He "leaned upon his braced arms while the shucks set up a terrific uproar beneath her thighs. Lying with her head lifted slightly, her chin depressed like a figure lifted down from a crucifix, she watched something black and furious go roaring out of her pale body. She was bound naked on her back on a flat moving car at speed through a black tunnel, the blackness streaming in rigid threads overhead, a roar of iron wheels in her ears" (*S* 268). *Light in August* treats the theme less directly, but Joe Christmas's first encounter with menstruation involves a similarly shocked discovery of the violation of static innocence. The young Christmas imagines menstruation as the flow of "something liquid, deathcolored, and foul" from what had at first seemed beautifully inviolable Keatsian urns (*LA* 178).

In *The Sound and the Fury* and *Sanctuary* the pictorial image and the tableau vivant (Caddy in the tree, Horace's first confrontation with Popeye) are still important expressive devices. Such techniques persist in *Light in August,* but they are increasingly subordinate to the representation of rhythm, pace, and velocity in things. Eating, speaking, traveling, remembering, lovemaking, and murdering are all presented as rhythms of the body or the mind. Even the mood of the crowd at Joanna Burden's fire-gutted house has its kinesic speech rhythm: "The women came . . . to print with a myriad small hard heels to the constant murmur *Who did it? Who Did it?* periods such as perhaps *Is he still free? Ah. Is He? Is He?* " (*LA* 273). The importance of pace and velocity is obvious in the contrasts between Christmas's running, Lena Grove's unhurried progress, Hightower's galloping fantasies, and Byron Bunch's workaday oblivion at the mill. Rhythm is also the crucial feature in representing several other figures, such as the furniture salesman who paces his tale about Byron and Lena to the rhythms of his and his wife's sexual responses.

As I Lay Dying is Faulkner's purest and most extreme representation of the world as motion. The novel is founded on an acceleration of the normal pace of life. A region that had been a place where "everything . . . hangs on too long" loses all stability and seems a "place where the motion of the wasted world accelerates just before the final precipice" (*AILD* 44, 139). The Bundren family gets caught up in a world in which everything is suddenly going too fast. The normally gradual process of adapting to change becomes the bridging of an abyss between one moment and the next. Such acceleration enables Faulkner to dramatize the existential ambiguities of position, continuity, and identity. As the Greeks knew, the phenomena of motion and change make all three of these concepts problematic. The implications of Heraclitus's question about stepping into the same river twice and of Zeno's motion paradoxes appear in the novel as psychic crises.

The most common images in the novel belong to the domains of topology and dynamics, the sciences of spatial relation and motion. The "space between us" is both psychic and physical; so is Anse's inertia (*AILD* 139). Motion and spatial relations are likewise the foundation of the two most pervasive image groups in the novel. These groups function differently from the imagery found in many multi-perspectival novels (including Faulkner's other ones). Each character draws on the same categories of imagery, and these categories thus serve as a sort of authorized lexicon for the fictional world. One group or category sets containers and surfaces against contents and depths, as in Dewey Dell's understanding of her pregnancy, Vardaman's vision of the "*is*" of Jewel's horse within its body, and Addie's notion of the word as a vessel (*AILD* 56, 55, 165). The other opposes vertical to horizontal, as in Anse's meditation on houses and roads or Addie's distinction between words and deeds (*AILD* 34–35, 165). Several material images reflect this latter opposition; blood and earth are horizontal, whereas air is vertical.

Like Darl imagining the family's journey as a flowing of the road past the unmoving wagon, the subject wants to think of himself as a stable entity in a fixed position. Likewise, he wants to think of his relationships to the significant others in his world as stable. This is especially so when the subject is largely constituted as a self by his relations to others, as is normally the case in Faulkner's mature fiction. Vardaman's selfhood, for example, is not a self-sufficient identity but a matrix of kinship relations, a position, as Faulkner later put it, in the "mosaic of the household" (*FU* 110).

All such relationshps are jeopardized in the accelerated world, however. All distances are increased, all differences are amplified, and all positions become isolated from one another. Real, material changes occur in the world at Addie's death and on the burial journey. The subject is asked to reexamine his relationship to the now alien objects in his environment and hence to reexamine his own selfhood as it is constituted by such relationships. The traumatized Vardaman must carefully ponder every change that appears in the family to determine if it has also altered him or the others or his kinship relations to them. "Cash has a broken leg. He has had two broken legs. . . . I haven't got a broken leg and pa hasn't and Darl hasn't and. . . . And Dewey Dell hasn't got a broken leg and I haven't. Cash is my brother" (*AILD* 186).

In the turbulent new environment no position or relationship can be taken for granted. Even the familiar, rural landscape becomes alien and threatening.[6] Addie's death in particular reveals ruptures in what had been supposed the continuous fabric of existence. These changes pose a number of questions to the Bundrens, questions which arise from the suddenly problematic concepts of self-identity and self-continuity. Who am I now, who was the child of an Addie Bundren who no longer is? If I am now different, what is the relation of the new "I" to the "I" who had a living mother? Is there a rupture in my existence as gaping as that between (Addie's) life and death? Complicating the situation further is the fact that Addie remains somehow alive to each of the Bundrens. All of them continue to refer to her in the present tense. Each is searching for a way to relate the awareness that she is dead to the equally valid awareness that something of her remains alive. Vardaman, for example succeeds fairly well at this for a while when he spontaneously makes a totemic identification of mother and fish.

The consequence of motion, then, is that the subject is faced with reestablishing relationship with everything in his world from which he has become estranged: the landscape, other persons, and the past selves from which the current self has somehow been born. The instrumentality of the technique is most apparent in Faulkner's invulnerability to such ominous consequences. On the one hand, the representation of fragmentary bits of consciousness is perfectly suited to expressing the threat of isolation and discontinuity. On the other hand, in order to represent the consequences of motion, Faulkner must exempt himself and his writing from

6. Cf. John K. Simon, "The Scene and Imagery of Metamorphosis in *As I Lay Dying*," *Criticism*, 7 (Winter 1965), 1–22.

them. The characters cannot be alien to the writer (or the reader) or separated from him by the abysses that divide them from each other. The impersonal representational technique, here the use of discrete interior monologues for the entire text of the novel, requires that the characters' minds be perfectly transparent to the writer and through him to the reader. The written text, the compositional activity necessary to have produced it, and apparently also the interpretive activity necessary to read it must remain outside the fictional world and invulnerable to the fluidity that governs it. That fluidity is not, however, a unique property of the fictional world but a representation of the real world, the one to which the text, its composition, and its interpretation belong. The technique thus fails to allow a place for its own existence; it belongs to a static realm, which the novel explicitly demonstrates as being impossible to maintain.

The transparency of the character to the writer is required as well in *The Sound and the Fury,* which uses a somewhat different kind of interior monologue, and in *Light in August,* most of which is written in the sort of indirect discourse in which the narrator voices the words of his characters. The enabling principle of such art is the writer's arrogation of a privilege that is regularly denied to his characters. Faulkner maintains perfect access to the minds of the others who are his characters and allows himself to travel the distances between them freely. Since the relationship with the other and the distances between selves are major themes in all Faulkner's referential novels, this can lead to an incongruity between the story and its telling. Such an incongruity is often the price willingly paid by novelists for flexibility of expression. The so-called omniscient narrator frequently exempts himself from the conditions governing the fictional world in order, for example, to show with clear-sighted perspicacity that the vision of his characters is necessarily flawed. For good reasons of its own, *As I Lay Dying* takes this incongruity to an extreme.

The anomaly between the story and the enabling principles of its representation becomes especially prominent in *As I Lay Dying* for two reasons. The first is that one of the characters, Darl Bundren, is allowed nearly the same representational powers as the writer. The chapters assigned to Darl are closer to third-person omniscient narration than any other first-person narratives I know of in Western literature. However, Darl must pay for his extraordinary access to the minds of others by going insane. No such consequence is demanded of Faulkner, who appears *in propria persona* only on the title page, or of the reader. The second reason is that, with the exception of this one striking anomaly, *As I Lay Dying* possesses the most internally self-consistent technique of any of Faulkner's novels. Faulkner, who continually pointed to the novel as a tour de force, a category about which he sometimes had mixed feelings, planned it this way from the outset.

> This would be a deliberate book. I set out deliberately to write a tour-de-force. Before I ever put pen to paper and set down the first word, I knew what the last word would be and almost where the last period would fall. Before I began I said, I am going to write a book by which, at a pinch, I can stand or fall if I never touch ink again. So when I finished it, the cold satisfaction was there, as I had expected.[7]

The novel's internal rigor requires some demonstration, for not all the book's critics have felt such cold satisfaction, particularly those who believe they have discovered inconsistencies in the time scheme or the narrative structure. R. W. Franklin, for example, has argued that several discrepancies exist between the point of action and the point of narration, that is, between the times at which the action occurs and at

---

7. James B. Meriwether, ed., "An Introduction for *The Sound and the Fury*," *Southern Review*, N.S. 8 (Autumn 1972), 709.

which the narrative utterance is performed.[8] M. E. Bradford suggests that such difficulties can be explained away, but only if we consider Addie (presumed to be the "I" of the title) as somehow the auditor of a novel which largely takes place after her death.[9] Numerous curiosities do indeed exist in the relation of the point of narration to the point of action, but these are precisely the crucial and distinctive aspects of the novel's technique. They express an essential condition of the text, the complex and daringly conceived relationship between events occurring in the fictional world and the phenomena represented by the language of the narratives.

Addie gives us the chief principle of the relationship when she insists that words and deeds necessarily diverge. A full discussion of the matter requires us first to examine her dissatisfaction with this state of affairs. "I would think how words go straight up in a thin line, quick and harmless, and how terribly doing goes along the earth, clinging to it, so that after a while the two lines are too far apart for the same person to straddle from one to the other" (*AILD* 165). Words and deeds (and the horizontal and vertical images associated with them) represent the two chief strategies in the novel for dealing with isolation and discontinuity. Each of them constitutes and expresses one kind of relationship to the world of events and to the kind of temporality found in that world. Addie is the one who *speaks*—the irony is significant—most vociferously for deeds and doing. She sees language as a medium of spurious relationships because it connects the speaker to things he cannot possess wholly and utterly. "We had to use one another by words like spiders dangling by their mouths from a beam, swinging and twisting and touching" (*AILD*164). The spider webs of language

8. R. W. Franklin, "Narrative Management in *As I Lay Dying*," *Modern Fiction Studies*, 13 (Spring 1968), 57–66.

9. M. E. Bradford, "Addie Bundren and the Design of *As I Lay Dying*," *Southern Review*, N.S. 6 (Autumn 1970), 1093–99.

establish connections, but connection is only a frustrating reminder of the distance remaining between Addie and the "secret and selfish life" of each of her pupils (*AILD* 162). She demands not connection or relationship at a distance but virtual consubstantiality. "Only through the blows of the switch could my blood and their blood flow as one stream" (*AILD* 164).

The fierce commitment to doing is an attempt to combat the isolation and meaningless of an existence which threatens to consist entirely of "getting ready to stay dead" (*AILD* 167). But only twice does the strategy prove successful. The first closing of the gap between self and environment occurs with the birth of her first child Cash. "My aloneness had been violated and then made whole again by the violation: time, Anse, love, what you will, outside the circle" (*AILD* 164). It is as if Cash were both a part of her own being and yet enough of an other that the fulfillment obtained in her relationship with him banished the rest of the world to irrelevance. The circumferences of self and environment coincide in the circle of her motherhood.

During Addie's affair with Whitfield, the other successful immersion in "the terrible blood, the red bitter flood boiling through the land," she lives so intensely in the immediate moment that she cannot conceive of anything outside of it, even when the affair suddenly ends (*AILD* 166). "But for me it was not over. I mean, over in the sense of beginning and ending, because to me there was no beginning nor ending to anything then. I even held Anse refraining still, not that I was holding him recessional, but as though nothing else had ever been" (*AILD* 167). To one who is completely immersed in the flood, only the present moment is real. Beginnings and endings are meaningless concepts unless one has the airy vantage from which to regard a past when anything else had ever been or a future when anything else might ever be.

But the affair does have an ending, as does Addie's exclusive relationship with Cash. A commitment to doing may forge intense continuities, but these are important. Time does matter. It only appears to be outside the circle until the second child is born or the lover goes away. The person who lies immersed in the flux of doing is defenseless against changes in the current.

The alternative strategy, one which is far more successful in coping with time, is tied to the way language is used by many of the narrators. To call the characters whose names appear at the beginning of each chapter narrators, however, is already to beg several important questions about the relation between the utterance and the person uttering. I use terms like narration, narrator, monologue, and speaker indiscriminately, but none of them is really adequate. Each presupposes a specific kind of intentionality on the part of the character to whom the utterance is ascribed. But the relation between the character and his words is precisely what is at issue.

One of the peculiar conventions established in the novel is a radical distinction between status of the past and present tenses. Faulkner invites attention to the distinction in several ways. He changes tenses within a single chapter quite frequently and often emphasizes the change with a shift in typeface. He also multiplies and accentuates the seeming anachronisms and discontinuities that perplex Franklin. One such signal of discontinuity is the placement of Addie's only monologue at a point in the novel when she has already been dead for five days. Another is Cash's casual reference to Mrs. Bundren's house in Jefferson, which points up a sudden break in narrative continuity and impels us to realize that Cash speaks from a time well after Anse's remarriage.

The passages in the various tenses usually seem to be uttered at the same time the events related in these passages occur. Several of Vardaman's and Dewey Dell's chapters read like particularly direct transcriptions of a stream of consciousness. Yet in spite of this appearance of immediacy, such chapters often paradoxically juxtapose more than one temporal perspective. Within what we supose to be a single, continuous utterance, events are regarded both as they happen and in hindsight.

Vernon Tull's account of Addie's funeral is like this. The events of the funeral itself are recorded in the present tense, seemingly as they take place, but this present-tense section is sandwiched between two passages in the past tense. The opening section perhaps brings the reader up to Tull's present time, the moment when Anse greets the funeral guests. If so, this only reinforces the impression of the simultaneity of funeral and its narration. Otherwise why should there be any change in tense at all? But at the end of a chapter, beginning in the middle of a paragraph, the point of view is suddenly sometime afterward, and events that take place three days after the funeral are narrated as past occurrences. Then with a shift in typeface but no change of tense, Tull relates an event which occurs on the drive home from the funeral.

There is simply no way for Tull's chapter to contain an immediate rendering of the funeral and also to be a single and continuous utterance, as even the paragraph divisions suggest that it is. The literal immediacy of the present tense is partially an illusion, occasioned by the special powers afforded in the novel to narrative language. Tull has the power to project himself verbally through time and space and to reenact the funeral as if it were immediately before him. He can do this with no cognizance of a discrepancy between the projecting subject reliving the events and the projecting subject, which is otherwise aware of such perilously relevant information as the fact that the burial journey is to be delayed far longer than anyone anticipates.

Such projections of the self occur frequently in the novel.

However, to the extent that projection necessarily implies a deliberate act, the term is misleading. When Vardaman tells of Darl's swim through the flooded river, the account of his own scurryings along the bank and of his concern for whether Darl has rescued the coffin appear in past tenses. But the moment when Darl emerges from the water empty-handed is in the present and is printed in italics (*AILD* 144). The grammatical and typographical distinction seems clearly a representation of Vardaman's involuntary state of mind. All the rest can be relegated to the mode of the passed and done, but the few seconds of painful recognition must be relived in their terrible immediacy. Vardaman's state of consciousness preserves as an "is" what must otherwise be "was."

Consciousness, then, can obliterate or refuse to recognize temporal and spatial distances, and consciousness in this novel is a phenomenon of narrative language. Words can cross the distances created by the flow of time and maintain events as permanently present. This power of narrative language is allied to a capacity to remain present that the characters attribute to words, sounds, and airy things in general. When the women at the funeral cease their keening songs, Tull supposes that the sounds remain in the air. "When they cease it's like they hadn't gone away. It's like they had just disappeared into the air and when we moved we would loose them again out of the air around us, sad and comforting" (*AILD* 86). Likewise, the sound of Cash's saw ceases, but it does not depart (*AILD* 71–72). Anse builds his house high on a bluff to assure its permanence. Even Addie, whose deeds must eventually boil away like the wild blood, remains a force after her death primarily through the "word" she has made Anse give her (*AILD* 119).

Darl is the most devoted practitioner of the strategy Addie opposes, the cultivation of the sort of consciousness expressed in present-tense narrative language. Like Addie's deeds, Darl's language is both expressive and constitutive; it both signals and establishes a relationship between subject and environment. Darl directs himself specifically against the force which defeats his mother, the "irrevocable" flow of time (*AILD* 139). He yearns at one point "to ravel out into time," an experience he imagines to be like the hypnotic state induced by watching the river (*AILD* 198). "It looks peaceful, like machinery does after you have watched it and listened to it for a long time. As though the clotting which is you had dissolved into the myriad original motion, and seeing and hearing in themselves blind and deaf; fury in itself quiet with stagnation" (*AILD* 156). But for the clotting of the self in one spatio-temporal position, Darl could unravel or dissolve into the whole of the environment. His apprehension of otherness would no longer be an experience of senses, which watch and listen from a single position. Dissolved into the river of time, the fury of the self's desires would have nothing to long for and no distant other to seek because the self would be present everywhere at once.

Darl is in fact able to move beyond the limits of the self with astonishing freedom. The ability is most apparent in the range and sensitivity of his narratives, where consciousness is most entirely free from the limitations of bodily location. The secret and selfish life of the other is open to his clairvoyant, telepathic consciousness. "It's like he had got into the inside of you, someway" (*AILD* 119). Neither space nor time can thwart the movement of such consciousness. Events that occur at different times and places, like Jewel's struggle to right the toppled lumber wagon and Addie's death the previous afternoon, can be simultaneously "is." Darl diffuses himself into the otherness of his environment so completely that, as both Anse and Dewey Dell notice, his eyes are "full of the land" (*AILD* 25, 35). Anse, in contrast, continually "looks out over the land" (*AILD* 19).

The introduction of such powers of consciousness into the novel and the establishment of present-tense narration as their medium are bold inventions. They belong to an art which is referential without being, in the everyday sense of conformity to normal verisimilitude, realistic. Consciousness is heightened and accelerated in the same way and for the same reason that the normal motion of the world is, to represent it more clearly. And just as Faulkner's immediate access to the minds of his characters is not really questioned in the novel, so the power of language to represent this consciousness goes largely unchallenged. The latter is a device, a literary technique, employed to enable Faulkner to make manifest the basic conditions of experience. According to the assumptions which the novel requires to make motion and its consequences visible—the assumptions that make the novel possible—one can establish in consciousness a relationship of virtual presence between subject and environment, and this relationship can be expressed perfectly in language.

The structural counterpart to such assumptions is the radical separation between the plane of action and the plane of narration. The individual monologues are not localized or represented as actions occurring within the novel's world at specific times and places.[10] The voices of the narrators arise from nowhere within the framework of the action; like the voices heard from the back porch of the Bundren house, "they sound as though they were speaking out of the air about your head" (*AILD* 19). In effect, each narrator might well have spoken as he lay dying. This division of the word from the act contrasts markedly with Faulkner's practice in subsequent novels, where he usually encloses the narrative

10. A few of the past-tense monologues are presented as if they were oral recitations and thus vaguely localized. Cf. Samson's references to himself as "talking now" and to what might happen "the day after tomorrow" (*AILD* 109, 112).

acts of the characters within the story and subjects them to the same kind of scrutiny as any other activity. In *As I Lay Dying,* narrative language is exempt from the conditions of the fictional world.

The language of the novel has no position in the world of events, suffers no isolation from it, and is not a part of its motion. Hence the oddity that this book, Faulkner's most detailed exploration of motion and fluidity, has the most static and crystalline form of any of his mature works. *As I Lay Dying* is indeed a tour de force of technical boldness and rigor. Hence also the restrained and lapidary quality of the style, which differs so greatly from Faulkner's later style, where the language strains and distorts itself in order to grasp an elusive reality just beyond expression.

But although the language of the novel is exempt, the characters whose consciousness it represents are not. If Darl's language is able to exist on an airy, insubstantial plane, Darl himself cannot. He is able to establish intimate and immediate relationships with the environment in his narratives, but his strategy is no more successful a means of coping with motion than Addie's. Darl's failure is related to his fearful refusal or neurotic inability to let "is" become "was." In consciousness all can remain an unchanging presence, but in the world of action the mules drown, Dewey Dell becomes pregnant, and Addie dies. The discontinuity between consciousness and the actual, material environment threatens Darl's sense of his own identity. " 'Then what is your ma, Darl?' I said. 'I haven't got ere one,' Darl said. 'Because if I had one, it is *was.* And if it is was, it can't be *is.* Can it?' 'No,' I said.' 'Then I am not,' Darl said. 'Am I?' " (*AILD* 95). Darl's consciousness diffuses itself into so many presents that he has not one identity, one "I am," but several. " 'But you *are,* Darl,' I said. 'I know it,' Darl said. 'That's why I am not *is. Are* is too many for one woman to foal' " (*AILD* 95). His ability to dissolve the clotted self almost amounts to a lack of self, as if he were draining his existence in the maintenance of the past's presence.

Just as Addie is unable to free herself from language and consciousness, much as she would like to identify being exclusively with doing, so Darl is unable to be free from his clotted bodily self, much as he would like to identify being with a clairvoyant *cogito*. The wish to dissove into the river of time is in effect a desire for the death of the bodily self, the acting and feeling Darl whose unreciprocated love for Addie and intense jealousy of Jewel root him in the here and now of the blood.

Darl's eventual breakdown reflects this division between a dispassionate, far-seeing consciousness and a physical and emotional self. Faulkner once suggested that Darl was mad throughout and that his madness was integral to his powers of consciousness (*FU* 113). It seems more accurate to say that the actual mental breakdown results from the incompleteness of those powers and from Darl's inability to be only the impersonal and virtually anonymous self of his monologues. He is sent to the asylum because he has acted, after all, not because he knows what a travesty the journey has become. Darl's final chapter displays even in its grammar a radically schizophrenic division between the calm, diffused consciousness and the intense, clotted self. The "I" who "knows" and "says" is disjoined from the bodily "Darl," also addressed as "you," who acts and is acted upon. "Darl" is placed on a train to the asylum in Jackson, but the "I" still floats freely to narrate the family's subsequent departure from Jefferson in the present tense. (*AILD*, 243–244).

Both Addie and Darl are seeking states similar to the absolute which is the goal of Faulkner's poetry. Each wants to abolish the distances between things in a world of motion by attaining some form of permanent presence in the relationship of subject and other. Darl succeeds in regarding the otherness of the environment as immediately present, but only at the cost of losing touch with his own selfhood. Addie is able to experience intense selfhood and on two occasions even to include the other in the circle of her aloneness, that fierce presence of the self to itself, but only at the cost of a frustrating alienation from the world at all other times. In fact, full and permanent presence is an unattainable condition in this and all of Faulkner's subsequent novels. Much of *As I Lay Dying* is devoted to demonstrating this, by establishing the partial successes possible for Darl's extreme, heightened commitment to the vertical and Addie's to the horizontal and then showing that the two directions are both incompatible and inseparable.

Darl's madness and Addie's resignation to life as a preparation for the permanence of death are not the only alternatives in the novel, however, because the desire for presence is not the only response to a world in motion. Anse, for example, does not respond in this way, and he has sometimes been seen as an early, rather unpleasant, embodiment of the Faulknerian virtue of endurance.[11] He is definitely an enemy of anything horizontal, precisely because horizontal prospects raise a frustrating and unsettling desire for otherness.

> When He [the Lord] aims for something to be always a-moving, He makes it longways, like a road or a horse or a wagon, but when He aims for something to stay put, He makes it up-and-down ways, like a tree or a man. And so he never aimed for folks to live on a road . . . because it's always men cant rest till they gets the house set where everybody that passes in a wagon can spit in the doorway, keeping the folks restless and wanting to get up and go somewheres else when He aimed for them to stay put like a tree or a stand of corn. [*AILD* 34–35]

11. Faulkner has himself lent some support to this view. See his comments in praise of how well most of the Bundrens cope with their fate, *Lion in the Garden*, 254.

Anse's self-centered inertia is a kind of wisdom in a world like this—"a wisdom too profound or too inert for even thought" (*AILD* 48)—but it is not a particularly happy alternative to the demand for presence. Nor are Dewey Dell's preoccupation with getting an abortion and Jewel's attention to his horse, both of these serving as fortuitous defenses against an awareness of distance and isolation, the kinds of action that can establish the subject in a general relationship to his environment. There is, however, another possibility in the use of language. Darl seeks to preserve experience as an "is" and drains himself in the effort. But language can also constitute the relationship to the past as a "was," thereby structurally acknowledging the gap between the "this was" of the narrated and the implicit or explicit "I say" of the narrating. Relationship is established and expressed, but it is relationship at a distance.

The relationship of a subject to the narrated past differs importantly from his relationship to a narrated present. Rather than looming as a contingent flux, the environment subsists as an hypostatized, quasi-objective phenomenon. The difference, of course, is not in the phenomena themselves but in the relationship established to them. Faulkner's characters sometimes directly witness the moment when the relationship changes and experience seems to precipitate out of the flux into solid, objectified events; in *Pylon*, for example (201): "When the reporter entered the twin glass doors and the elevator cage clashed behind him this time, stooping to lift the facedown watch alone and look at it, he would contemplate the inexplicable and fading fury of the past twenty-four hours circled back to itself and become whole and intact and objective."

By definition the perception of experience as objective necessitates a critical detachment from it. For Darl, as for Vardaman, the death of his mother is an experience from which he cannot or will not detach himself. However, most of the characters outside the family and occasionally those inside it can view the events of their world from a critical perspective and in the past tenses. That there is an ontological gap between themselves and the events is no particular cause for alarm, because the gap is not by itself threatening to the identity of a man with the self-justifying powers of a Whitfield. In Jean Pouillon's terms, the outsiders have knowledge of events: "We will never understand Faulkner's point of view unless we distinguish between consciousnes and knowledge. . . . Consciousness is inevitable, knowledge only a possibility. . . . Chronology, being a posterior organization of a life, belongs to the domain of knowledge. It is a kind of intellectual liberation from destiny; it assures us that the past is indeed past even if we feel its pressure on our present."[12] In *As I Lay Dying* the two kinds of verbal relationship to experience, consciousness and knowledge, generally diverge. Consciousness is subjective but impersonal, since the self is raveled out into the environment it is conscious of. Knowledge is objective but personal, the relationship of a discrete self to a discrete environment.

The divergence of consciousness and knowledge helps explain the often disquieting experience of reading *As I Lay Dying,* for the reader is always encourged to entertain both relationships. When Vardaman bores holes in the face of his mother's corpse, we necessarily share Vardaman's consciousness of the doing as a tender expression of love and concern and also the outsider's knowledge of the resulting deed as a desecration. The two understandings are as incompatible as they are mutually unavoidable. The same doubleness enters into the long and unresolvable critical debate over whether the Bundrens' journey is more epic heroism than bizarre travesty.

12. Jean Pouillon, "Time and Destiny in Faulkner," Jacqueline Merriam, trans., *Faulkner: A Collection of Critical Essays,* Robert Penn Warren, ed. (Englewood Cliffs, N.J. 1966), 83.

Another way of defining the divergence is to say that, far more than consciousness, knowledge allows a moral response to experience. The opinion is more dogmatic than his novels always justify, but Faulkner has argued that moral judgment is alien to immediate participation in experience:

> Life is not interested in good and evil. Don Quixote was constantly choosing between good and evil, but then he was choosing in his dream state. He was mad. He entered reality only when he was so busy trying to cope with people, that he had no time to distinguish between good and evil. Since people exist only in life, they must devote their time simply to being alive. Life is motion and motion is concerned with what makes man move—which is ambition, power, pleasure. What time a man can devote to morality, he must take by force from the motion of which he is a part. [LG 252–253]

With the partial exceptions of Tull and Peabody, who are significantly the only non-Bundrens to make much use of the present tense, all the outsiders place the doings of the Bundrens in bounded moral categories. All express decided opinions on the either/or questions of what is right and wrong, proper and improper, or sane and insane. The opinions of some—Cora Tull and Whitfield—are comically hypocritical and imperceptive, but those of Mosely, Samson, and Armstid are entire common sense. Regardless of the degree of moral sensitivity that a particular outsider may have, however, none of them is able to express in a past-tense narrative the sense of immediacy, contingency, and fluidity which is the common denominator of the burial journey as experienced from the inside.

Cash, the only Bundren who narrates primarily in the past tenses, does have the ability to appreciate experienced contingency, however. In the chapter recounting Darl's commitment to the asylum, Cash makes the only real effort in the novel to reconcile consciousness and knowledge. Cash, who insists on building "on the bevel," is also the only character who functions well on both the horizontal axis of deeds and the vertical axis of words (*AILD* 77). According to a widely accepted interpretation, this humane and mature flexibility is a triumphant virtue in the novel. Yet the deep anxiety expressed in Cash's last two monologues betrays the fact that the victory has its cost.

Throughout the novel Cash has tried to conquer his personal anxieties by busying himself with things he can measure and shape to precision, such as the coffin he builds for Addie. Dewey Dell recognizes that his skillful carpentry is a way of transforming the flux of time into solid, controllable forms. "And Cash like sawing the long hot sad yellow days up into planks and nailing them to something" (*AILD* 25). When the injury to his leg bars him from such constructive activity, he turns to language to express himself. But here too he is reaching for verbal planks to measure and join.

Cash's narrative is a dialogue between consciousness and knowledge, or more accurately, an attempt by the latter to insist that its objectivity overrides the subjective misgivings of the former. The colloquialism of his opening sentence begins the attempt: "It wasn't nothing else to do" (*AILD* 222). He doesn't say there wasn't anything "I" could do but uses instead an impersonal construction that removes all subjectivity from the event. The decision to put Darl away is hypostatized as an "it," thus transforming what had been contingency into destiny. The knowledge that the decision was by community standards the only right response to the burning of Gillespie's barn is apparent to Cash, but he still has considerable misgivings. Thus he looks for justification in the common-sense objectivity of the group, acquiescing to the opinions of "the balance of us," "the majority of us," "other folks," and "most folks," rather than deciding for himself (*AILD* 223).

Attempting to treat such a tormenting experience as objective still does not answer his doubts, however. As he recalls the anguished moments when the decision was made and when Darl realized that Cash too had betrayed him, he seeks nostalgic refuge in metaphors from the precise world of carpentry. These things are unequivocally objective, and a man can know what's right and wrong. "Folks seems to get away from the olden right teaching that says to drive the nails down and trim the edges well always like it was for your own use and comfort you were making it. It's like some folks has the smooth, pretty boards to build a courthouse with and others dont have no more than rough lumber fitten to build a chicken coop. But it's better to build a tight chicken coop than a shoddy courthouse" (*AILD* 224). The analogy is splendidly irrelevant, as Cash recognizes sadly. "And when they both build shoddy or build well, neither because it's one or tother is going to make a man feel the better nor the worse" (*AILD* 224). The contingent flow of experience does not admit of precise measurement and well-trimmed edges any more than it admits of either/or moral categories.

Cash's monologue is a tissue of hesitations, equivocations, and contradictory statements. He is unable to align the necessity of objective knowledge with his awareness that the burning of the barn and Darl's mental state are not discrete judicable phenomena. They are part of a baffling complexity which includes the entire journey, the suspect motives of Jewel and Dewey Dell, and especially Cash's own bond with Darl. Cash is acutely aware that he has been his brother's silent accomplice. "It looked like one of us would have to do something. . . . And me being the oldest, and thinking already the very thing that he had done" (*AILD* 223–224). Even when he thinks about the situation afterward, he can "almost believe" Darl "done right in a way," and so he is forced to suspect that he has grievously betrayed his brother by acquiescing to the community's objectivity (*AILD* 223). But knowledge can not quite accommodate itself to this, and so he is forced to conclude by doubting the objective knowledge his entire monologue has been devoted to establishing. "But I aint so sho that ere a man has the right to say what is crazy and what aint. It's like there was a fellow in every man that's done a-past the sanity or the insanity, that watches the sane and the insane doings with the same horror and the same astonishment" (*AILD* 228). Cash is able to recognize and name that fellow, a man's impersonal consciousness, but he is not quite able to constitute it in the structure of a past-tense narrative.

Cash's monologue is an embryonic version of the next phase of Faulkner's art. Unlike the other narrators, Cash consciously calls into question the ability to represent the world accurately. His attempt to accommodate consciousness and knowledge, distance and presence, and horizontal and vertical is in many ways the most satisfactory response to a world in motion developed in the novel. But it raises its own problems, ones which necessarily remain on the periphery. *As I Lay Dying* is primarily devoted to representing motion as it is immediately apprehended and to demonstrating the divergence of a world so perceived from a world of stable, objective events and entities. In trying to reconcile the two ways of establishing relationship to the world, Cash undertakes the task of shaping experience truthfully. He wants to understand experience both as a dynamic flow and as something in which objective forms and patterns can be found. He is only partially successful at the task, but his attempt anticipates the more sustained efforts to solve the same problem in *Absalom, Absalom!* Unlike most of the other monologues, Cash's narrative is a dynamic verbal performance. It is a kind of action as well as an instrument of expression. Significantly, Cash makes the only address in the novel to a reader-figure, the "you" is "outside of it" (*AILD* 226–227). This anchors his language in a rhetorical context, thereby serving to separate it from the rootless, free-floating language common to the rest of the novel. Out of Cash's series of rhetorical improvisations and tentative assertions, which contradict previous ones without replacing or repudiating them, eventually comes, in the next phase of Faulkner's career, a new narrative technique and a new attitude to technique as such. To replace the transparent and instrumental means of representation used in Faulkner's referential novels, the next phase of his career seeks a form open not only to worldly experience but to the treacheries of its own ongoing attempt to shape experience.

5

The Fate of Design

As I Lay Dying and *Absalom, Absalom!* occupy parallel positions in Faulkner's career, each of the novels a development of one aspect of the concept of arrested motion. The former, as we have seen, is Faulkner's most sustained consideration of the theme of motion. The latter is his most sustained meditation on the activity of arresting. In the referential fiction the characters and the writer himself are also both perforce engaged in arresting motion. *Absalom, Absalom!*, however, marks a significant change in Faulkner's understanding of this characteristic artistic activity. The change can be broadly described by saying that the labor of representation is for the first time in *Absalom, Absalom!* made a part of the text. The novel accordingly puts in question just those referential premises that had enabled Faulkner to write the works of the previous phase. As we shall see in analyzing *Absalom, Absalom!*, this change in turn opens the way for new questions about the purpose of art and its place in the world.

The question of arrest turns in part on the relation of subject to object. Arresting is the means by which the subject represents the object, that is, the world in motion, to himself. Faulkner's understanding that the aim of every artist (and the typical desire of every character) is to arrest motion by artificial means allows for an abrupt distinction between subject and object. The subject can exercise the power to be detached from the world and to regard it as if from across a distance. In the referential fiction the writer always maintains such detachment, and so, frequently, do the characters. Cash's impersonal consciousness, which watches the sane and the insane doings of the world, is one example. There are a number of others throughout Faulkner's work, in which a character seems to watch the world indifferently—the customary word is "muse"—from the other side of a barrier.

In such instances the techniques of arrest and the resulting forms and concepts by which motion is structured constitute the barrier. Such forms give the subject a means of shaping and processing experience and also of coping with it. For the characters, however, these forms often prove ineffective either as defenses against the turbulent motion or as ways of organizing it. The subject's detachment from motion serves at best to postpone a breathless immersion in it. For example, all of the principals in *Light in August* (but for Lena Grove, who never supposes herself aloof from motion) discover that they cannot maintain their detachment. Hightower's dream of foolhardy glory, Byron Bunch's clock-ordered regimen, and Christmas's desperate flight from society all prove unable to limit motion or to keep the world at bay.

For such characters, the measure of the success of their forms of arrest seems to be a fairly simple one, the adequacy of the form in balancing between the external fluidity and an internal need for stasis and order. For a character to be without adequate means of structuring experience is for him to be threatened by a kind of vertigo in the face of unmediated and therefore incoherent fluidity. At night Ike Snopes cannot even "see and know himself to be an entity solid and cohered in visibility instead of the uncohered all-sentience of fluid and nerve-springing terror" (*H* 188). Benjy Compson experiences a similar vertigo at the welter of chaotically whirling shapes which appear when he is put under ether and when he is drunk on the wedding champagne. Such moments of crisis for the two idiots are the extremes of formlessness in Faulkner's writings; motion is not arrested at all but experienced with terrifying immediacy.

The common failing among other characters is the opposite, a need for rigid and static forms in which to contain, to understand, and thus to cope with worldly experience. Horace Benbow and Quenton Compson are ready examples of characters who try to barricade themselves against life's motion by refusing to acknowledge all that' does not conform to their subjective ideals. Such characters are just as vulnerable to vertigo. Throughout Faulkner's career the climactic recognition scenes depict the panic of such a character at the sudden breakdown of his mental constructs before a flood of menacing experience. The scene in *Sanctuary* in which Horace gazes at the photograph of his niece is an example. A later one is Levine's suicide in *A Fable*.

Yet although the character's attempt to shape and limit the motion of the world usually proves ineffective and his detachment from the world only illusory, Faulkner in the referential novels constantly maintains his own detachment from motion. The impersonal artist gives the appearance of coolly selecting or inventing the artificial forms that arrest the motion of the world in his text. His relation to the world and to the text is one of mastery over an external thing. The first criterion for the writer's success seems to be the same as for the character's ability to cope with motion. Successful literary forms strike a balance between the fluid disorder of the world and the transcendent stasis of the writer's viewpoint. The difference is that the writer's stasis is never seriously threatened by the fluidity across the barrier. His detachment from the world and his mastery over it allow the striking of a balance to belong to the purest and most sanitary formalism. Craft and technique are only "tools," as Faulkner sometimes later called them. [1] They can be picked up or discarded as the occasion demands, without ever being invested with any real existential significance to the writer or any power over him.

The situation is never quite this simple, to be sure. Even in the referential fiction, success in striking a balance between order and disorder or stasis and motion is only the most elementary measure of a writer's forms and techniques. The point is that even this elementary measure becomes highly problematic in *Absalom, Absalom!* In that novel the writer's arrest of motion is no longer allowed to depend even initially or primarily on the formalistic, emotionally neutral deployment of tools.

The novel also insists upon one of the writer's tasks in arresting motion which goes beyond those he shares with Darl Bundren and Quentin Compson. In addition to coping with the motion of the world, the writer seeks to make an artifact which will represent that world. Arresting and shaping as the work of creating a product—a dynasty, a historical narrative, or a book—are central to *Absalom, Absalom!* as they never are in the novels of the previous phase. Only in such isolated incidents as the furniture dealer's story in *Light in August* do the characters of the referential novels seek to produce narrative accounts of the world like their creator's.

The term in *Absalom, Absalom!* which gathers the several meanings of arrest, production, and form is "design," Thomas Sutpen's word for his plans and ambitions. The word can be construed in three different ways, as an *intention*, an *act*, and a *pattern*. Each of these is relevant to the novel and to its significance in Faulkner's career. A design is first an intention toward that which is to be shaped; Sutpen and his chroniclers all have designs upon the material before them. Used in this way, the noun signifies the pre-existing rela-

1. For some of Faulkner's uses of tools and carpentry as metaphors for literary technique, see *Faulkner in the University*, 3, 239, 257.

tionship between a designer and his material. As a verb, design stands for the act of shaping, Sutpen's continuing implementation of his plans or the narrators' struggles to produce an account of his life. And finally, again as a noun, a design is a result, the shape the designer has produced or the pattern into which he has transformed the material.

The problem of design in *Absalom, Absalom!* manifests itself in the seeming failure of every attempt at it. Sutpen's intention to create a dynasty ends in ruin; the narrators' attempts to shape Sutpen's story are confused and uncertain; and Sutpen and the narrators all confess their failure to find a pattern that will allow them to explain what has happened. Quentin, after insisting that Shreve would have to be born in the South to understand, admits that he doesn't understand either (*AA* 361–362). Rosa Coldfield has for forty years been asking *"Why and Why and Why"* (*AA* 170). Mr. Compson confesses of his own design for the story that "it just does not explain" (*AA* 100). Even Sutpen admits in the bifurcated account of his life to General Compson that he can't discover his mistake (*AA* 267–268).

In the earlier fiction the analogy between the arresting activities of the characters and those of the artist is largely a way of conceiving the significance of human endeavor. In *Absalom, Absalom!* the direction of the analogy is reversed. The representation of the characters' attempts to shape their own lives and, especially, to compose narrative accounts of experience becomes a way of interrogating art. Faulkner does not here exempt himself, as he does earlier, from the conditions that govern his fictional world. His representational activities are not privileged over those of his narrators, nor does he adopt the impersonal, Godlike viewpoint which had characterized the earlier novels. Sutpen's design is a crucial part of the novel's self-interrogation, but the most immediate question for the writer is the relationship of the narrators' designs and the design of the novel. What is at stake in designing a narrative, and why are the characters so unable to compose one that satisfies them? Can the novel be said to succeed where the narrators have failed, and if so, what would it mean for the novel's design to be called successful? What, in short, is the measure of successful design?

The mere asking of such questions marks a change in Faulkner's career, for it draws into the open the enabling principles of the previous phase. As I suggested in the previous chapter, *Absalom, Absalom!* is in part an exploration of questions uncovered in the closing pages of *As I Lay Dying*. A rather tidy developmental logic connects Cash's final monologues to the concern in *Absalom, Absalom!* with composing an account of past—rather than immediate, ongoing, and incomplete—experience. But the links between the two novels bespeak more differences than similarities. The most important premise of *As I Lay Dying*, the writer's ability to represent fully the inner lives of his characters, is what the writer and the narrators seem least able to assume in *Absalom, Absalom!*

Although by Faulknerian standards of verisimilitude, *Absalom, Absalom!* is a realistic enough novel—probably more so than *As I Lay Dying*—it is not particularly a referential work in the sense in which I have been using the term. It is not simply an impersonal representation of a theme, the question of design, which happens to be more self-reflexive than Faulkner's earlier themes. (The theme is not in fact noticeably more reflexive or self-referential than some of the themes in *As I Lay Dying*. However, the earlier novel's concern about language really operates only at the level of the characters' representational activities.) *Absalom, Absalom!* is not, in other words, an imitation of the question of design as rhetorically posed by a writer who yet stands behind his novel in serene and confident mastery and by this stance refuses the application of the question to his own design.

Rather, the asking of the question demands the establishment of a new set of relationships among the writer, his
material, and the particular design of his text.

Although we can be reasonably sure that the narrators'
designs fail, it is not so easy to say where the inadequacies lie.
They are not particularly to be found in the patterns that
govern each narrator's account. As Olga Vickery has shown,
these patterns are in large part those of distinct literary
genres: Greek tragedy, the Gothic tale, and chivalric romance.[2] Mr. Compson's version of the story can perhaps be
criticized as too willfully rigid an application of the form of
Greek tragedy, but he is the first to point out that his design
is unsatisfactory. More interestingly, the pattern itself is far
more compelling than Mr. Compson is ever allowed to say.
Faulkner admitted as much years later when he identified
Sutpen's destruction with "the old Greek concept of tragedy" (*FU* 35).

Mr. Compson's narrative founders on the arbitrariness of
casting Charles Bon as an embodiment of fate. Compson
calls him an "effluvium of Sutpen blood and character" in a
desperate attempt to make sense of his "impenetrable and
shadowy character" (*AA* 104). But of course he is more
than an effluvium; we eventually learn that he is Sutpen's
repudiated black son and thus a perfectly convincing representative of the nemesis necessarily raised by by Sutpen's
hubristic design. A similar case can be made for the adequacy of Rosa's Gothic demonizing. Faulkner originally
planned to entitle the novel "Dark House," and its Gothic
machinery is not solely a product of Rosa's imagination (*SL*
78–79). The burning of Sutpen's mansion, for example, is

2. Olga Vickery, *The Novels of William Faulkner,* rev. ed. (Baton
Rouge, La. 1964), 84–102. For an attempt, which I find unconvincing, to
distinguish Shreve's "tall tale" from Quentin's "romance," see Lynn G.
Levin, "The Four Narrative Perspectives of *Absalom, Absalom!" PMLA,*
85 (January 1970), 35–47.

an appropriately Gothic conclusion which she never gets to narrate.

Rosa's demonizing expresses her need to relegate Sutpen to the realm of the supernatural, and this need derives chiefly from what she insists is the one lasting outrage he has committed against her. Raised to consider him an ogre and later deeply shocked by his proposal for a trial breeding, she asserts to Quentin that she has nonetheless forgiven him all but one thing, his having died and thus put himself forever beyond the reach of her questions. Sutpen as demon is thus not so much the definitive pattern Rosa affirms for the story as the "zero signifier" she invokes for the inexplicable excess of meaning in it.[3] Or rather, to use a term more appropriate to Rosa's sensibility, "demon" serves her in much the same way the trope "infinity" serves Poe, Rosa's most illustrious Southern predecessor as a sentimental poet and teller of Gothic tales. "This, like 'God,' 'spirit' and some other expressions of which equivalents exist in all languages is by no means the expression of an idea—but of an effort at one. It stands for the possible attempt at an impossible conception."[4]

Mr. Compson's design for the story uses fate—"Fate, destiny, retribution, irony—the stage manager, call him what you will" (*AA* 72–73)—in the same way, as a sign of the inexplicable. The uncanny machinations of fate are for Mr. Compson the very pattern of the events, even as he admits: "It's just incredible. It just does not explain" (*AA* 100). He, in fact, uses inexplicability and his own failure to explain as the confirmations of his design. "Or perhaps that's it: they dont explain and we are not supposed to know. . . . You bring them together again and again nothing happens: just the words, the symbols, the shapes themselves, shadowy

3. Claude Lévi-Strauss, "Introduction à l'oeuvre de Marcel Mauss," in Marcel Mauss, *Sociologie et anthropologie* (Paris 1966), xlvii.

4. Edgar Allan Poe, "Eureka," *Complete Works* (New York 1902), XVI, 200.

inscrutable and serene, against that turgid background of a horrible and bloody mischancing of human affairs" (*AA* 100–101).

The patterns that Mr. Compson and Rosa offer for the story are simultaneously forms which confess their failure to find a truly satisfactory form and designs which are more cogent than either narrator is able to say. This anomalous situation may suggest to us that the essential criteria for design are to be found not in the patterns but in the personal limitations of the designers and the ways in which they apply otherwise compelling forms. In a statement often quoted as an authoritative commentary on the novel's status as an exercise in multiple perspective, Faulkner argues just that.

I think that no one individual can look at truth. It blinds you. You look at it and you see one phase of it. Someone else looks at it and sees a slightly awry phase of it. But taken all together, the truth is in what they saw though nobody saw the truth intact. . . . The old man was himself a little too big for people no greater in stature than Quentin and Miss Rosa and Mr. Compson to see all at once. It would have taken perhaps a wiser or more tolerant or more sensitive or more thoughtful person to see him as he was. It was, as you say, thirteen ways of looking at a blackbird. But the truth, I would like to think, comes out, that when the reader has read all these thirteen different ways of looking at the blackbird, the reader has his own fourteenth image of that blackbird which I would like to think is the truth. [*FU* 273–274]

Read as an epistemological credo, the statement gives with one hand what it takes away with the other. Faulkner begins by asserting a radical relativism: no one can see truth. But he also characterizes the novel as a way of overcoming relativism. The reader is supposed to do what no individual can. And the writer, who reassures us in these words that some whole truth exists, necessarily commands the same powers to comprehend truth, just as he does in *As I Lay Dying*.

Read less rigorously, as a suggestion of the moral qualities one needs to design a true image, the statement points
to other difficulties. Perhaps the reader (and the writer) can
be expected to be wiser or more tolerant than Shreve and
Quentin, say, who have much the same task as the reader in
assembling a composite image out of "old tales and talking"
(*AA* 303). To read Faulkner's statement in this way encour-
ages us to give over looking for truth in designs and images
themselves; it licenses us to scrutinize instead the moral
qualities inherent in how the narrators go about their acts of
designing. By understanding their personal failings, we can
be expected to be directed toward nobler and more effective
methods of composing a fourteenth image. Again this suggests the mode of *As I Lay Dying* or *The Sound and the Fury,*
where the reader is allowed to share the writer's objectivity
and to inspect from above the failings of Addie's or Jason's
strategies for arresting motion.

Such modes of analysis, however, are likely to lead to the
uncomfortable conclusions reached by James Guetti in a
study which is otherwise the most thorough consideration of
the problem of design in this novel.[5] Although he does not
cite Faulkner's comment about the fourteen ways, Guetti
pursues the arguments that both an epistemological and a
moral reading of it would suggest. He insists that Faulkner
means to show in the novel the necessary and inevitable failure of design—in Guetti's terms, of metaphor. *As I Lay Dying* can, for example, surely be said to demonstrate the inevitable failure to arrest the motion of present experience and
to offer a reasonably full explanation of why it is inevitable.
But Guetti finds that failure in *Absalom, Absalom!* results on
the one hand from unexplained and perhaps inexplicable
premonitions of failure, silence, and darkness and on the
other from the idiosyncratic qualities of the designers. In

5. James Guetti, *The Limits of Metaphor* (Ithaca, N.Y. 1967), 69–109.

both cases Faulkner's own design is flawed. Either the writer cannot articulate the significance of the darkness that Guetti shows to be an essential part of both Quentin's and Sutpen's imaginations, or else the novel speaks only of the circumstantial and thus finally insignificant difficulties that these particular unwise, intolerant, and insensitive narrators find themselves in and so offers the reader precious few insights about how to design successfully.

The gap between a vague but universal failure of design and one that seemingly proceeds from very specific but local and unrepresentative circumstances—Mr. Compson's want of information, for example—is the result of the paradox Guetti wants to see at the heart of the book, a paradox which is a version of the Cretan liar's dilemma. According to Guetti, Faulkner means to design a novel which demonstrates that all designing fails. But Faulkner's own inevitable failure produces an incoherent text that Guetti must reluctantly conclude is "no novel at all."[6]

Looking for the failure of design either in the narrative patterns or in the character of a narrator and the way this conditions his act of designing produces readings that show, directly or indirectly, the similarities between *Absalom, Absalom!* and the more univocally referential works. Both kinds of analysis finally objectify the text; that is, they examine it as a self-contained second world which has a relatively straightforward mimetic relationship to our primary world. There are many good reasons for reading *Absalom, Absalom!* in this way, and I do not mean to suggest that, for example, to read the novel as a fictional representation of Southern history will lead one inescapably into logical paradox. My purpose in suggesting the limitations of such analysis is to clarify by contrast the difference between the enabling assumptions of *Absalom, Absalom!* and those of earlier novels. Rather than

6. Guetti, 108.

assuming or stipulating a relationship between the world of the text and the world of reality, Faulkner in *Absalom, Absalom!* is specifically trying to *establish* such a relationship. But this relationship proves to be as risky and uncertain as the one between the South, which Quentin is asked to tell about, and the narrative of the Sutpen family he offers in response.

The enabling assumptions of *As I Lay Dying* include a first world discovered to be significant because of men's attempts to arrest its turbulent flow, an instrumental language which can represent men's consciousness of the world, and a writer who is able to detach himself from the world in order to represent it objectively and impersonally. *Absalom, Absalom!* questions all these assumptions. It does so partly by insisting upon the remaining meaning of design: design as intention, or rather as the intentional relationship between the designer and his material, the designs he has upon it and those it has upon him.

One aspect of the circumstantiality that bothers Guetti is in fact a crucial element in this relation between designer and material. It is precisely the local, in William Carlos Williams's sense of the term, which grounds the problem of design and removes it from the realm of abstract formalism. To the characters in the referential novels, by contrast, the question of arrest usually is abstract. Darl Bundren's attachment to "some concept, some shape of beauty" is precisely the desire to subordinate the concrete local detail to an abstract form (*FU* 110).

In *Absalom, Absalom!*, for the writer as well as for the characters, the local is what pre-exists the self, what is inherited from the past. As I pointed out in the previous chapter, to regard the past is to be faced with something no longer characterized by motion. Cash and the narrators of *Absalom, Absalom!* are seeking to design a flux that has solidified or precipitated. The past assumes the aspect of something substantive or material. And in becoming material, the past

becomes much the same kind of thing as the worldly literary materials which a writer engages.

For Faulkner the two essential properties of literary material are just these. Literary material is a substance, and it is
inherited by the writer because of his living in a certain time
and place. Both properties are crucial to the problem of
design. Faulkner often insists on the materiality of what he
has been given to write about. His material is the South,
"my little postage stamp of native soil," a body he invariably refers to in synechdocal figure as land and earth and soil
(*LG* 255). The image is not of men's doings or a historical
tradition or a culture but of the land itself. In *Absalom,
Absalom!* the image is on virtually every page: the "tranquil
and astonished earth" which Sutpen overruns (8), the "land
or earth or whatever it was that destroyed Sutpen at last"
(12), the "land" which Sutpen advises the Klan to attend to
if the South is to be saved (161), and even the Continental
Trough which links Quentin and Shreve: "that River which
runs not only through the physical land of which it is the
geologic umbilical, not only runs through the spiritual lives
of the beings within its scope, but is very Environment
itself" (258)

Language, the writer's medium, is itself an inherited materiality. In a pair of early essays Faulkner contrasts what he
sees as the meager achievement of the American writer with
his fortunate situation as the heir to the "wealth of natural
dramatic material in this country, the greatest source being
our language" (*EPP* 89).[7] American speech has a distinctively "earthy strength" that the writer must learn to appropriate (*EPP* 89). In this otherwise ordinary metaphor, language itself appears as palpably material and thus a quite
different thing from the transparent medium of representa-

7. The two essays, both from 1922, are "American Drama: Eugene
O'Neill" and "American Drama: Inhibitions," *Early Prose and Poetry*, 86–
90, 93–99.

tion it is in *As I Lay Dying*. The failing of American literature, Faulkner asserts, is that it is as yet "inarticulate" (*EPP*
89). The earthy material has not yet been well articulated,
not yet properly divided up and set in order. Such an inadequacy is a failure of design.

Each of these concepts and images operates in *Absalom,
Absalom!*, where the difficulties of appropriating one's material inheritance are explored in full. To exist in the world of
the novel, for example, is to be *"a certain segment of rotted
mud,"* or a *"narrow delicate fenced virgin field,"* or *"articulated
flesh"* (*AA* 171, 326, 166). All of the narrators find in the
Sutpen story material intimately connected with Southern
heritage. For Quentin especially, this heritage prominently
includes the language in which it is bequeathed to him;
everyone, it seems, *"sounds just like father"* (*AA* 181). The
story itself is primarily a tale of inheritances. Sutpen and his
descendants all live in a world where fathers customarily
bequeath difficult burdens to their children.[8]

The central problem of design in *Absalom, Absalom!* is the
relationship between a designer and an inherited body of
material, a relationship that largely constitutes both the material and the designer as such. Subject and object exist not
as truly independent entities but by virtue of a relationship
which defines them both. Quentin is not "a being, an entity" but a "commonwealth," the sum of his relationships
to the "ghosts" of the past (*AA* 12). He never really con-
fronts the material for a first time but only remembers it.
*"But you were not listening, because you knew it already, had
learned, absorbed it already without the medium of speech somehow from having been born and living beside it, with it, as children will and do: so that what your father was saying did not tell
you anything so much as it struck, word by word, the resonant*

8. For an important psychoanalytic reading of this theme in both of
the novels in which Quentin figures, see John Irwin, *Doubling and Incest/
Repetition and Revenge* (Baltimore 1975).

strings of remembering" (*AA* 212–213). Likewise, for Rosa Coldfield the *"unpaced corridor which I called childhood"* and the "Cassandralike listening beyond closed doors" which figuratively portray the relation to her inheritance have taught her *"to listen before I could comprehend and to understand before I even heard"* (*AA* 144, 60, 140). The common situation of Sutpen in trying to establish a dynasty, of Charles Bon in seeking the recognition of a father, of Quentin Compson in trying to tell about the South, and of the writer in composing a novel is to exist by virtue of an already established relationship to inherited material.

From the point of view of the designer of a life, a historical recitation, or a novel, this relationship is the way in which he apprehends his inherited material before he actually begins to design it. This mode of apprehension is what I have also called the intention of a design and what Husserlian phenomenology would designate more rigorously as an intentional structure.[9] It largely determines the fate of design as act and as pattern. For example, Mr. Compson's act of casually designing the tale as an amusing if somewhat bizarre after-dinner story and the tragic pattern he finds in it both belong to the relationship already established between him and the Southern past. From the outset he assumes his own age to be permanently alien to the simple and foolhardy heroics "of that day and time, of a dead time; people too as we are, and victims too as we are, but victims of a different circumstance, simpler and therefore, integer for integer, larger, more heroic and the figures therefore more heroic too, not dwarfed and involved but distinctive, uncomplex" (*AA* 89).

The novel's most important image of a relation to what pre-exists poses Sutpen and Quentin directly against the inherited materiality of earth. For Sutpen at the moment his

9. Cf. Edmund Husserl, *Ideas: General Introduction to Pure Phenomenology*, W. R. B. Gibson, trans. (London 1931), 121–123, 241–244.

design is born, the earth is a "limitless flat plain" against which his "innocence" rises "like a monument" (*AA* 238). (This scene is the closest thing in the book to a representation of the primordial moment when the relation between designer and material initially gets constituted.) In contrast, Quentin, as he rides out to the Sutpen house with Rosa finds himself enclosed within the substance of his world and thwarted by it.

> The dustcloud in which the buggy moved not blowing away because it had been raised by no wind and was supported by no air but evoked, materialized about them, instantaneous and eternal, cubic foot for cubic foot of dust to cubic foot for cubic foot of horse and buggy, peripatetic beneath the branch-shredded vistas of flat black fiercely and heavily starred sky, the dust cloud moving on, enclosing them not with threat exactly but maybe warning, bland, almost friendly, warning, as if to say, *Come on if you like. But I will get there first; accumulating ahead of you I will arrive first, lifting, sloping gently upward under hooves and wheels so that you will find no destination but will merely abrupt gently onto a plateau and a panorama of harmless and inscrutable night and there will be nothing for you to do but return and so I would advise you not to go, to turn back now and let what is, be.* [*AA* 175–176]

These two images of a character's relationship to earth depict also the two necessary and reciprocally opposed relationships to materiality of the novelist himself. The first, utter detachment from material which is assumed to be so much unformed and pliable stuff, is an assumption of mastery. It allows the writer to command his material just as Sutpen speaks "the *Be Sutpen's Hundred* like the oldentime *Be Light*" (*AA* 9). The second is a recognition of helplessness, a realization that one does not speak the material so much as listen to it and be spoken by it. The writer in composing the novel—as the composing of the novel—enacts both relationships. He is at all points trying to effect "some happy marriage of speaking and hearing" which might surpass the differences between them (*AA* 316). If the text stands as that marriage, however, it is more truly an amalgamation of the two relationships than a synthesis of them into a third, encompassing perspective.

The only place where the differences between the two relationships do seem truly to be surpassed is the one region where they have not yet come into being, the mountain paradise where Sutpen is born. There in a country beyond history and almost beyond culture—if culture be defined as differentiation, categorization, and articulation—one's relationship with land is harmonious, "because where he lived the land belonged to anybody and everybody" (*AA* 221). The young Sutpen "had never even heard of, never imagined, a place, a land divided neatly up and actually owned by men" (*AA* 221). What is at stake in design—Sutpen's, Quentin's and the writer's—is possession. As in *Go Down, Moses* the initial possession of the land is the origin of history and civilization. It is the act of original sin, Promethean theft, and godlike creation which founds the opposition between nature and culture.[10] For the writer, to whom this opposition appears as that between his material and what he makes of it, as that between reality and fiction, the composition of the novel is his attempt to take possession of the material for fiction.

Sutpen's story begins with a fall from the communal Eden. (The mythic interpretation is explicit in the narrative Quentin has inherited from his grandfather.) On the journey down to Tidewater Virginia the earth itself seems to be the agent transforming Sutpen's relation to it: "They did not seem to progress at all but just to hang suspended while

10. For a discussion of the logical distinctions between nature and culture and an analysis of how this has figured in the work of Lévi-Strauss and other structuralists, see Anthony Wilden, *System and Structure* (London 1972), 245–272.

the earth itself altered" (*AA* 224–225). The fall and the new relation to earth reveal two things to Sutpen. One is the fact that he has a heritage which conditions his own life: "All of a sudden he discovered, not what he wanted to do but what he just had to do, had to do it whether he wanted to or not, because if he did not do it he knew that he could never live with himself for the rest of his life, never live with what all the men and women that had died to make him had left inside of for him to pass on, with all the dead ones waiting and watching to see if he was going to do it right" (*AA* 220). The other is the specific character of his inheritance from his poor-white father as one of the "cattle, creatures heavy and without grace, brutely evacuated into a world without hope or purpose for them" (*AA* 235).

Both these discoveries arise out of his being turned away from the plantation owner's door, and they result eventually in his lifelong endeavor to repudiate the inheritance and replace it with one of his own design. That endeavor is of course an act of awesome and hubristic will, but it is important to note that the exercise of will and the design itself both follow the establishment of a relationship between self and substance which then allows the will its freedom. The young Sutpen's final discovery in his lengthy debate with himself proceeds from the conclusion that no relation at all exists between himself and the plantation owner to the vision of earth as a *tabula rasa*. "*There aint no good or harm either in the living world that I can do to him.* It was like that, he said, like an explosion—a bright glare that vanished and left nothing, no ashes nor refuse; just a limitless flat plain with the severe shape of his intact innocence rising from it like a monument" (*AA* 238). The designing will finds room in which to work only with the belief in its self-contained alienation from the social order and with the corresponding belief that the world is but clay in wait of the sculptor's tool or a blank page awaiting inscription.

These beliefs are the foundation of Sutpen's innocence and the enabling principles of his design. Sutpen's relationship to the limitless flat plain never changes; he continues to believe from then on that material—the land, the social order, other persons—can be shaped according to his design. "It was that innocence again, that innocence which believed that the ingredients of morality were like the ingredients of pie or cake and once you had measured and balanced them and mixed them and put them into the oven it was all finished and nothing but pie or cake could come out" (*AA* 263). Even as the narrator of his own life story Sutpen is aloof from the material, almost indifferent to it: "He was not talking about himself. He was telling a story. He was not bragging about something he had done; he was just telling a story about something a man named Thomas Sutpen had experienced, which would still have been the same story if the man had had no name at all, if it had been told about any man or no man over whiskey at night (*AA* 247).

This passage accurately depicts also the intentional relationship between writer and material in the referential novels. It is undoubtedly more truthful to say, however, that it describes the result, in which the writer has achieved the desired impersonality, than his process of composition. Even in 1933, only two years after he had proclaimed the value of impersonality and four years after he had written *As I Lay Dying,* his most impersonal work, Faulkner argued that the process of writing could never be impersonal for a Southerner. "That cold intellect which can write with calm and complete detachment and gusto of the contemporary scene is not among us."[11] Sutpen's desired mastery over his material nevertheless duplicates and puts in question the apparent mastery of *As I Lay Dying.* It might be argued that

11. James B. Meriwether, ed., "An Introduction to *The Sound and the Fury,*" *Mississippi Quarterly,* 26 (Summer 1973), 412.

Sutpen represents only an extreme exaggeration of the will to power over one's material, but Faulkner has upon occasion expressed a similar hubris. "I can move these people around like God, not only in space but in time too" (LG 255).

The failure of Sutpen's design shows the inadequacy of such a relationship to material. Sutpen's relationship is, in fact, not simply inadequate but false to the actual state of affairs. Contrary to his beliefs, Sutpen cannot help but be related to the plantation owner and to the social order represented by him. Likewise, the land is not a *tabula rasa*. The proof of Sutpen's error lies in the double bind that follows upon his attempt to vindicate the little boy at the door (AA 274). He can only make sure that any "nameless stranger" and his descendants are welcomed in and thus "riven forever free from brutehood just as his own (Sutpen's) children were" by turning away his eldest son (AA 261). The instruments with which he combats the plantation owner—"land and niggers and a fine house" (AA 238)—are not neutral materials with which he can create a cosmos out of the "soundless Nothing" (AA 8). They are not, that is, like the tools Faulkner sometimes thinks his literary techniques to be. They are materials which have already been designed and which retain the power to shape the user in their own image. Sutpen even seems for a moment, as Quentin tells it, to realize the shaping power of materiality when he speaks of needing "to have what they have that made them do what the man did" (AA 238). The supposedly neutral materials, in other words, prove to be the implements of a social order that Sutpen necessarily winds up repeating rather than repudiating or transforming.

Quentin has no such innocence about the materials of his heritage. His relationship to the ghosts of the Southern past dictates not that he design them but that they design him in their own image. If Sutpen's freedom to design his life is largely an illusion founded on his innocence about the power of inherited materiality, Quentin's "freedom" is "that of impotence" (*AA* 12). He can only recognize help-lessly that he has been made into the "Quentin Compson who was still too young to deserve yet to be a ghost, but nevertheless, having to be one for all that, since he was born and bred in the deep South" (*AA* 9). The other Quentin Compson also, the one "preparing for Harvard," who may yet have some hope of designing his own life, discovers that even in Massachusetts he cannot escape "listening, having to listen" (*AA* 9). "*I am going to have to hear it all over again I am already hearing it all over again I am listening to it all over again I shall have to never listen to anything else but this again so apparently not only a man never outlives his father but not even his friends and acquaintances do*" (*AA* 277). This passage fol-lows Quentin's protest to Shreve that "I am telling." But Quentin's fate, one he comes to recognize fully, is always to listen to the material and never to speak it.

Quentin is so often and so casually referred to as the princi-pal narrator of the novel, especially of the second half of the book, that it is important to recognize just how little he speaks. Excluding what is merely thought and seen by Quen-tin but uttered by the third-person narrator and ignoring remarks of a sentence or two, Quentin "speaks" only 60 pages of the 378-page novel. What Quentin does say is re-peatedly characterized as second- or thirdhand transmission of the words of his father, General Compson, or Thomas Sutpen. All of his spoken narrative is in chapter VII, where he punctuates his discourse with "father said" and "grand-father said" so frequently that Shreve virtually parodies him at one point. "I see. Go on. And father said—" (*AA* 266). Cleanth Brooks's chart of the main conjectures made about the Sutpens reveals the same thing. Only one of the forty or so can be attributed to Quentin.[12] Quentin does, after some

12. Cleanth Brooks, *William Faulkner: The Yoknapatawpha Country* (New Haven 1966), 432–436.

resistance, assent to the romance motif introduced by Shreve, but he never really offers a pattern of his own. In fact, with the crucial exception that his story is meant to *"tell about the South,"* he can hardly be said to intend a design at all (*AA* 174).

But of course a design does get spoken in his share of the novel. In one respect it is a conglomeration of all the ghostly voices which have spoken previously. Yet Quentin's design emerges most fully from the scenes that he alone cannot help but hear and see. "He could see it; he might even have been there. Then he thought *No. If I had been there I could not have seen it this plain"* (*AA* 190). The power of Quentin's relationship to material is that he is so deeply enclosed within it and submitted to it that he can see and know it more intimately than anyone else. Only Quentin can discern the element that most fully explains the story, the secret of Bon's birth. Many critics have been bothered that this knowledge seems to have no source.[13] They usually want to see the discovery of the secret conform to the kind of designing they understand Quentin to be practicing, "that best of ratiocination which after all was a good deal like Sutpen's morality" (*AA* 280). Such critics are therefore forced to assume that Quentin has been told by Henry or Clytie and that Faulkner somehow neglected to inform us of this most essential incident. But as Shreve realizes, Quentin learns of Bon's identity just by entering the house for the first time and standing face to face with one of Sutpen's children. "She didn't tell you, it just came out of the terror and the fear after she turned you loose. . . . She didn't tell you in the actual words because

13. Among the many essays in which the problem of the source of Quentin's knowledge is raised, see John Hagan, "Fact and Fancy in *Absalom, Absalom!" College English*, 24 (December 1962), 215–218; Aaron Steinberg, "*Absalom, Absalom!:* The Irretrievable Bon," *CLA Journal*, 9 (September 1965), 61–67; and Floyd C. Watkins, "What Happens in *Absalom, Absalom!?" Modern Fiction Studies*, 13 (Spring 1967), 79–87.

even in the terror she kept the secret; nevertheless she told you, or at least all of a sudden you knew" (*AA* 350–351).

Intimate knowledge of material comes only from submitting oneself to it and being shaped by it. Quentin's passivity, his "sullen bemusement," is as necessary for a successful design as the power of will exercised by Sutpen and belatedly even by Rosa, who "refused at the last to be a ghost" (*AA* 280, 362). Whereas Sutpen's assumption of mastery over the earth allows him the will to design it but at the same time constitutes his "purblind innocence," Quentin's awareness of the "weightless permeant dust" moving "sluggish and dry across his sweating flesh" allows him the power of vision and forecloses the power of will (*AA* 280, 362).

What is at stake in the question of design is the possibility of successfully appropriating one's heritage. It is apparently not possible to refuse the question. Bon, who at first thinks that "no man had a father," discovers that he must spend his life seeking recognition from a father "out of the shadow of whose absence my spirit's posthumeity has never escaped (*AA* 299, 317). Bon and Henry represent another important pair of relationships to inheritance, the one seeking to establish recognition that he has a father and the other borne down by the burden of a father's command. For the writer, however, the problem of design is chiefly manifested in Quentin and Sutpen.

In one respect the problem of design and inheritance is a theme represented in the novel by the actions of the Sutpens, Coldfields, and Compsons. But the novel is not only the representation of action but a kind of action itself, the enactment of the writer's appropriation of the South as literary material. Both submitting to his material and striving to establish mastery over it, Faulkner seeks to make it his own in a way quite different from that he had peremptorily used in the referential novels. The boldest assertion in the book is the signature to the map in its endpapers: "William Faulkner: Sole Owner and Proprietor." As the inscriptions on this map make clear, the act of appropriation extends beyond *Absalom, Absalom!* to include all the Yoknapatawpha County fiction yet composed. It extends even into the future in the reference to the then unpublished (and probably unwritten) story of Flem Snopes as a bank president. But the confidence displayed on the map should not obscure the fact that *Absalom, Absalom!* presents a kind of art in which the writer's proprietorship over his material is less likely to be secured than strived for or at best tenuously maintained.

The crucial problem of design in the novel, then, is not the detached writer's deployment of forms that can adequately mediate between order and disorder. It is the prior question of establishing a relationship to one's material which then makes the use of such forms possible but which at the same time forecloses the possibility of true detachment. In Geoffrey Hartman's terms the writer's relation to the *genius loci* takes priority over his relationship to Genius.[14] The writer's relation to native materials and his capacity both to command them and to submit to the claims they make upon him takes precedence over form as such and over the writer's place in a tradition of literary forms.

Absalom, Absalom! and most of the novels that follow after it differ from the referential works in a number of prominent ways. The three most important of these are all related to the new centrality of the writer's relationship to inherited materials. The first is the significance of history. Faulkner's reputation as a writer who is obsessed with the past may obscure the fact that he is, until 1936, chiefly a novelist of the contemporary scene. Until *Absalom, Absalom!*

14. Geoffrey Hartman, "Towards Literary History," *Beyond Formalism* (New Haven 1970), 356–386. See my discussion of these ideas in Chapter 1.

history figures in the novels primarily as a background against which his characters strive to cope with the motion of the contemporary world. But nine of the eleven novels published after 1935 are wholly or largely historical, and they are centrally concerned with taking possession of an inheritance or with relinquishing one.

Another difference, which first appears in the 1935 *Pylon,* is Faulkner's adoption of a new style, the one that is normally and rightly thought of as characteristically Faulknerian: the use of long sentences and complex, suspended constructions. As Faulkner explained a number of times, the style is his attempt to get the past into the present. "A man, a character in a story at any moment of action is not just himself as he is then, he is all that made him, and the long sentence is an attempt to get his past and possibly his future into the instant in which he does something" (*FU* 84). In other words, the style is explicitly a means of taking possession of the past. Moreover, it serves the writer as a means of personally appropriating his material. Whereas the ideal in the referential works had been artistic impersonality and the style had accordingly been much less of a signature, a characteristic style is by definition personal, even in Faulkner's case idiosyncratic. It manifests the writer's necessarily personal attempt to take possession of his material and to mark it permanently as his own.

The final and most important difference is the relation of the representational act to the resulting representation. In *Absalom, Absalom!* the result, the finished book, includes the act, the attempt to take possession of the material and to shape it in some definitive form. Rosa Coldfield, the only character in the novel who is a writer, gives us several metaphors for the act of representation and describes the attendant relationships among designer, material, and designed product when she speaks of *"that sickness somewhere at the prime foundation of this factual scheme from which the prisoner*

*soul, miasmal-distillant, wroils ever upward sunward, tugs its
tenuous prisoner arteries and veins and prisoning in its turn that
spark, that dream which, as the globy and complete instant of its
freedom mirrors and repeats (repeats? creates, reduces to a fragile
evanescent iridescent sphere) all of space and time and massy earth,
relicts the seething and anonymous miasmal mass"* (*AA* 143). The
achieved dream—a dynasty or a work of art—is necessarily
a mirror and a repetition of the massy earth. But it is not
created primarily to be a truthful representation or an object
of aesthetic contemplation. It is the means by which the
prisoner soul strives to create itself as a free and distinct
being. Like Thomas Sutpen, the writer struggles to create
himself and his freedom as distinct from the anonymous
earth and connected to it by a relation of mastery. But, like
Quentin, he knows also that he must always remain a prisoner of that massy materiality and that he cannot create a
new earth, only repeat the old one in fragile, evanescent,
iridescent sphere.

One may read an exalted conception of art in Rosa's
words; it lies in the capacity of art to attain a kind of permanence. The prisoner soul *"dies, is gone, vanished: nothing,"*
but its representation of the earth "relicts" the material in
permanent form (*AA* 143). Faulkner's use of "relict" as a
verb has a precise function here. It combines two related but
distinguishable ideas. One is the notion of giving something
up and getting free from it; "relinquish" is the word
Faulkner normally uses for this idea by itself. The other is
the notion of leaving behind a relict which survives. The
prisoner soul thus makes a survivor of the representation as
he leaves it and the massy earth behind.

In repeating the world, giving a design to its material and
arresting its motion in the palpable form of a house, a social
structure, or a novel one leaves "a mark on something that
was once," which may then pass to the "stranger" Judith
speaks of in giving Bon's letter to Mrs. Compson (*AA* 127).

The stranger has the name and the same function, it seems, as the stranger who is to read Faulkner's novels one hundred years hence, according to the 1955 definition of art as arrested motion. In fact, art is for Faulkner man's most permanent "creation of something . . . which will outlast him" (*LG* 103). A man "can't live forever. He knows that. But when he's gone somebody will know he was here for his short time. He can build a bridge and will be remembered for a day or two, a monument, for a day or two, but somehow the picture, the poem—that lasts a long time, a very long time, longer than anything" (*LG* 103).

Such lofty sentiments as these likely seem quite at odds with the bleak tone of *Absalom, Absalom!*. But the novel is, in fact, made primarily according to principles of design which would allow for such a belief in art's power. The principles I have been explicating do not, however, go unchallenged in the novel. Having traced Faulkner's ideas about proper design from the initial and relatively simplistic notion of form as a balance between stasis and fluidity to the more paradoxical requirement that the writer must both speak his material and be spoken by it, we must now pay attention to those aspects of the novel that call the paradoxical requirement into question. A further scrutiny of Rosa's words in the passage quoted above will show how *Absalom, Absalom!* opens itself to a critique of the principles it otherwise firmly maintains. Her words undercut the novel less directly than do Cash's in *As I Lay Dying,* but they serve the same function in pointing the way to the problem on which the next moment in Faulkner's career will center. What comes into question is not the method of design but its purpose and its consequences.

Rosa is not talking about art in the passage I have quoted but rather of her own reluctance to face the sickness somewhere at the prime foundation of things. She is at this point firmly committed to the "*might-have-been which is more true than truth,"* that is, to a romantic dream which entirely escapes such striving against massy materiality (*AA* 143). The struggle against materiality which she deems herself incapable of is also a highly romantic notion, and we must ask whether the novel supports it fully.

The most problematic aspect of Rosa's discourse is her depiction of earth as a chaotic, formless materiality. The concept resembles Sutpen's assumptions about earth, except that Rosa sees materiality not as a neutral resource but as an almost actively malevolent and corrupt miasma. Unformed materiality cannot really be corrupt, however, because there is no such thing as a primal miasma in *Absalom, Absalom!* One's material inheritance is always already inscribed with the cultural designs made upon it by earlier prisoners: designs that include the incest taboo, the plantation system, and Greek tragedy. The question that plagues Quentin, after all, is not how to design an adequate representation of the Sutpen story or even how to understand it, but how to live amid the dusty wreckage of the designs which have been bequeathed to him. The continuing malign power of these designs over his life and the similar power of already existing designs over the lives of Sutpen and his family suggest that the carriers of corruption are designs themselves, not materiality. The sickness is to be found not at the prime foundation of things but in the productions and representations that may ensue from the struggle with materiality.

If this is so, Faulkner's sentiments about the permanence of art are not so much lofty as frightening. Writing a novel like *Absalom, Absalom!* may answer the methodological question with which we began—how to design successfully—but writing a novel that represents and thus repeats sickness may be only a way of transmitting the disease. The permanence of art may be not a virtue but a crime, for it perpetuates the contamination more effectively even than Sutpen's abortive dynasty.

Rosa's language thus leads to a new problem of design, one which ultimately needs to be seen in a context wider than that of this one novel. To recognize that designs may themselves be diseases that infect the generations to come is to have moved beyond the initial question about how one might design successfully. This question is answered, though only in paradox, by the exploration of the intentional relationship to inherited materiality. One must somehow both speak it and be spoken by it. The text of *Absalom, Absalom!* is itself an answer to this question to the extent that it advances a considerable distance toward the paradoxical goal in its circling, tortuous, and fully self-aware articulations.

The new problem is primarily a question neither of one's relation to materiality as such nor of whether that materiality is conceived to be formless, pliable, corrupt, or already potent with design. The intentional relation to materiality is the one which makes new designs and productions possible, and the enabling power of this relationship generally continues to be assumed throughout the rest of Faulkner's career. The new problem is the relationship between designs, the relationship, that is, between one's own productions and the forms of the past. To recall Hartman's distinction once more, this is the writer's position with respect to Genius. Faulkner now begins to ask if there is some way in which one's own designs can be more than a perpetuation of past forms and a conveying into the future of whatever disease they carry. He asks the question, for example, through Ike McCaslin, who in *Go Down, Moses* tries to escape the curse his ancestors' designs have brought upon the land.

Mildly comforting replies to such a question can be seen in the two novels which follow *Absalom, Absalom!* Bayard Sartoris in *The Unvanquished* does manage to transform the code of violence that his father and the war have bequeathed to him. More ambiguously, Harry Wilbourne in *The Wild Palms* manages to proclaim bravely that *"between grief and*

nothing, I will take grief" (324). But in *Absalom, Absalom!*
itself the fate of design is always ruinous. Most of the characters in the novel are faced with the same predicament as
the writer; all need to produce designs that will have a
healthy relationship to the designs of the past. Sutpen, who
recognizes the design of the plantation system but thinks he
can replace it with his own creation, winds up repeating it
instead. Quentin, who is fully aware of the designs of the
past and the power they wield, remains silent and unpro-
ductive in an attempt to avoid accepting such tragic knowledge. Sutpen's heirs, especially the descendants of Charles
Bon, are generally ignorant of their situations as inheritors
of the design. Their lives are merely dispersed across the
land and without a witting relation to a past or a future;
they grow up without fathers and their sons are all soon
orphans.

The designs of the past thus get furthered in *Absalom,
Absalom!* in exactly the ways which I argued in Chapter 1
are the principal threats to a healthy career; repetition, silence, and dispersion. The parallel is no coincidence. The
fate of design and the trajectory of a career are fundamentally similar phenomena; both operate as historical processes
and as open systems. Their essential mode of being therefore includes a relation to the past and a relation to the
future. The recognition of this parallel between a literary
career and social and cultural history is the foundation of the
next phase of Faulkner's writing. By considering in this
next phase the fate of a particular culture's designs, Faulkner
in fact raises the course of his own career to the level of an
explicit theme in his fiction.

6

Elegy as Meta-Fiction

The final and longest-lasting episode in Faulkner's career begins with the publication of *The Hamlet* in 1940. The episode has a somewhat different relation to its predecessors than, for example, the referential phase has to the visionary one. Earlier changes in the program of the career, as we have seen, can be understood as challenges to the enabling principles of the immediately previous phase. In the concluding phase, however, Faulkner seeks more to preserve and further what has been won in the earlier writings than to expose their questionable premises. The Snopes trilogy, our exemplary text in this chapter, attempts to comprise all of what has gone before and, most importantly, to find a new level of organization for it rather than to dismantle the assumptions necessary to *Absalom, Absalom!*

The most significant point on which the works after 1940 do challenge the ones before is that of the relation assumed to exist between interior consciousness and the external world. The later novels extend still further the persistent trend we have noticed in Faulkner's writings toward closing the gap between subject and object. In Faulkner's poetry the consciousness of the individual subject is almost always detached from the tawdry material world, even to the point of a visionary solipsism. The detachment is somewhat more compromised in *The Sound and the Fury* and *As I Lay Dying,* but the principal issue in those novels remains the individual's attempt to cope with the bewildering motion of experience. In *Absalom, Absalom!* the issue passes more directly to a problematics of arresting. As this happens, the aloofness from the world which Thomas Sutpen assumes is challenged and largely supplanted by the more primordial distinction between subject and materiality. Consciousness and materiality come into being at some mythical, originating moment but only in an intentional relationship to each other. From then on the *cogito* which Addie Bundren and the Quentin of *The Sound and the Fury* had treasured for itself is copresent with a material *cogitatum*, which it intends and is intended by.

As we have seen, even this primordial subject/materiality distinction is challenged in *Absalom, Absalom!*, but it is never quite given up. The novel calls into question the possibility that the world can ever have been the shapeless earthiness that Sutpen and Rosa conceive it to be. However, just as the epistemology implicit in Cash's monologues quietly interrogates the assumptions of *As I Lay Dying* but comes to be fully exploited only in *Absalom, Absalom!*, so the challenge to the dominant structure of the subject/object relationship in *Absalom, Absalom!* serves primarily as a seed for the next phase of the career.

The distinction between consciousness and raw materiality is largely abolished in the last phase. The subject there is always already in a world and constituted by his relation to it. We noticed in the last chapter an important similarity between Faulkner's two prominent mentally retarded characters, Benjy Compson and Ike Snopes. There is an important difference also. Unlike Benjy or the other Compsons and Bundrens at moments of crisis, Ike in his daily moment of early morning terror is not detached from the fluidity of experience but indistinguishable from it. Even when he is without his minimal social identity and without an awareness of his bodily existence, he still finds himself to be inseparable from the world's "uncohered all-sentience" (*H* 188). Ike is at such times more utterly bereft of pre-existing structures than any other character in the late fiction. More typical are the moments immediately following, when the visible world returns and he finds himself belonging, like all the other characters, to a world of already arrested motion, a world of previously established designs that have already made their characterizing marks upon the individual and do not allow him the kind of withdrawal of consciousness into itself which had been available to each of the Bundrens. In such a world arrest and motion are not clearly distinct phenomena, the one a property of mind and the other of external experience. Rather, the individual is from the outset part of a world constituted by their relationship, constituted, that is, by already established forms which in turn help to determine the individual's subjectivity. Flem Snopes is always already inside a world of cultural forms and institutions which direct his power to desire and to act. Even Ike McCaslin, who wants to break with the world he has inherited, can imagine doing so only by exchanging it for the even more structured world of the wilderness. "The Bear" may be Faulkner's great nature poem, but in it he makes clear that nature is in a sense more like civilization than civilization itself, because nature is even more strictly a world of established custom and ritual.

Such customs and rituals make up the principal theme of the concluding phase of the career. Almost all the novels of Faulkner's last decades address a single, complex problem: the fate of design. What, they ask, are the consequences of the diverse organizations of experience which the human sciences variously refer to as codes, structures, patterns, designs, forms, fictions, and myths? *Absalom, Absalom!*, *The Unvanquished*, and *The Wild Palms* all at least implicitly raise the same problem, the consequences of the personal, cultural, and literary fictions which men produce, for those who come after as heirs (Quentin Compson and Bayard Sartoris) or for those who survive the collapse of the fictions they have lived by (Harry Wilbourne and the tall convict). The problem is a more specific version of a concern which has never been absent from Faulkner's prose and which in the works between 1940 and 1962 often becomes thematically explicit: how to endure, how to go on when the structures we have made of experience prove inadequate. The question is made more urgent by the knowledge that burdens Quentin and his creator in *Absalom, Absalom!*, the knowledge that all such structures are flawed and that even so they may continue to exert a crippling pressure on subsequent generations. Immediately and expressly at stake in the last phase is the possibility of surmounting the despair which has claimed Quentin.

The themes of the late fiction are not new ones for Faulkner, although he now frames them somewhat differently and extends them into wider contexts than the fate of an exemplary protagonist. Faulkner is still asking how we are to distinguish good designs from bad. Which ones will allow us to go on, and which will prove as lethal as Thomas Sutpen's, John Sartoris's, and Charlotte Rittenmeyer's? In the more openly didactic spirit of the late fiction, these questions can be fairly described as posing the problem of values. What are values, and how are they found or made? What is their relation to the cultural designs and discursive structures that literary fictions subsume, investigate, and transmit? Almost every major character in the works after 1940 is directly seeking either to challenge or to maintain existing value systems and the institutions in which they are embodied. In addition to the characters of the trilogy and those such as Charles Mallison and Gavin Stevens who also appear prominently in other works, one can point to Ike McCaslin, Lucas Beauchamp, Nancy Mannigoe, and all the principal characters in *A Fable*.

The concept of value is common to the study of language and the study of wealth.[1] In the Snopes trilogy Faulkner's continuing attention to the structures of language and of social discourse is joined by and then fused with an increased attention to the structures of economic interchange. He understands that in all these areas the question of value concerns the bonds between persons which are made when they exchange words, commodities, and sexual favors and also that these bonds find their most important manifestations in cultural patterns, social and economic institutions, and literary fictions. Value, then, is ·the term that denotes the character of such bonds and the quality of the relationships they establish.

The concern for the consequences of design and for the values which are institutionalized in social structures directly implicates the work of the writer. As we began to see in the last chapter, it calls into question his responsibility for the literary fictions he produces. Though Faulkner continues to announce that he writes without regard for the possibility that his books will be read, in practice his fiction is at this time directly concerned with its relationship to readers and to the culture in general. (During these same years Faulkner allows himself to become a public figure and a spokesman for both his region and his nation: he begins writing essays and public letters, he tours several parts of the world for the State Department, and he speaks at length about his writing and his personal views in classroom talks and interviews.) The writer has discovered himself to be a purveyor of values, and he now requires himself to attend to the consequences of the ones he transmits, transforms, or criticizes in his writing. In this as in some other ways Faulkner steps

1. Ferdinand de Saussure's recognition of this analogy between economics and language is one of the founding principles of modern linquistics. See the *Course in General Linguistics,* Wade Baskin, trans. (New York 1966), 79–81.

aside from that aspect of modernist ideology in which aesthetic matters generally prevail over moral ones or are at least understood to be clearly distinguishable from them. He returns openly to the belief in the inextricability of moral and aesthetic concerns characteristic of many earlier writers, including the nineteenth-century realists. Hence all the talk in the 1950s about truth, which though it rarely is as interesting as any of Faulkner's fiction, has proven revealingly embarrassing to critics who wanted to hear about form and technique. Faulkner now rejects the impersonal stance he had employed in *As I Lay Dying.* Where he once set himself the pure task of representing a character such as Jason Compson, a task that did, of course, have moral implications, now he expressly devotes his attention to what one may do about such a character as Flem Snopes.

For the writer to take such responsibility for the values treated in his work implies that he believes the written word to have considerable power. And it is true that even characters in Faulkner's fiction who are otherwise aloof from the written word and indifferent to strictly literary texts find themselves acting at key points on the strength of a book or making appeals to textual authority. Thomas Sutpen begins his career by going to the West Indies; his only knowledge of them comes of hearing a recitation from a book he is not yet capable of reading. *The Wild Palms,* where Faulkner repeats the strategy of Cervantes, Flaubert, and Twain in opposing true fiction to false, deals explicitly with the power of the written word and the responsibility of the writer. The tall convict's rage at the pulp writers who have deceived him is comical, of course, and we might be inclined to ignore its impact if it did not reinforce Harry and Charlotte's reliance on nominally more respectable writers.

Written texts are likewise important in *Go Down, Moses.* Appeals are made to the Bible and to a Keats ode. The crucial texts in that novel, however, are nonliterary: the newspaper article in which Molly Beauchamp wants her grandson's death reported, Lucas's imaginary treasure letter, and the bills of sale, checks, marriage licenses, and bills of divorce on which the rest of "The Fire and the Hearth" turns. Preeminent among these nonliterary texts is the McCaslin plantation's commissary book, whose entries of credit and debit form "two threads frail as truth and impalpable as equators yet cable-strong to bind for life them who made the cotton to the land their sweat fell on" (*GDM* 256). Compared to such a document, a fictional narrative seems to have little significance as a text in which the bonds between persons may be represented.

This is the other way the writer's work is called into question, for its place in a culture which does not seem to need storytelling. Faulkner asks in particular what the relation of narrative to culture may be. The question has two aspects. On one side stands the writer's role as a critic and a promulgator of cultural fictions, fictions that men do indeed live by. This is, in the language of the arrested motion paradigm, his responsibility to the stranger a hundred years hence. On the other side stands the marginality of his work for the very people he is writing about. The writer thus takes on a double burden in seeking to relate his work to the culture at large, for he knows both that the fictions he is writing about have real consequences and that his own books are read only infrequently by those whom they most concern.[2]

2. In a 1946 letter to Malcolm Cowley, in which Faulkner mentions, as he had before, the particular marginality of art in Southern society, he adds the observation that this is the case because the South did not possess a literate middle class until well into the twentieth century. When this class did appear, Faulkner suggests, it came of a union between the old gentry and the ambitious small farmers who had migrated to the towns (*SL* 215–217). The birth of this class and hence of a native readership is, in fact, a minor theme in the trilogy. Its chief representatives are Charles Mallison, as tutored by V. K. Ratliff, and Linda Snopes, as tutored by Gavin Stevens. (For these observations I am indebted to an unpublished paper by Peter Petrie, which traces the theme in *The Hamlet*.)

Of the two strategies Faulkner tries for addressing his culture and speaking about its values, far the more troubling is the method of didactic allegory used in *A Fable*. Like most other critics, I consider the novel a failure, but I am also not sure that anyone has yet read it thoroughly and properly. The book so differs from Faulkner's other mature works as to suggest that he was deliberately attempting to step outside the discipline otherwise evident in his career. More than anything else he wrote, *A Fable* asks to be understood as a summary text, a final statement on a question no less imposing than "what is man?" (Throughout the writing of the novel Faulkner seems to have expected it to be his "last major, ambitious book."[3]) Consequently he seems to ignore the lesson about the application of abstract designs to human behavior which *Absalom, Absalom!* (among others) had explicitly demonstrated.[4] Instead he chooses an allegorical pattern, the Passion story in conjunction with the tomb of the unknown soldier, then attempts to erect a story around it.[5] This use of such patterning is very different from that in *The Sound and the Fury* or *Light in August,* where the sometimes almost whimsical traces of a Christian pattern are clearly supplementary to something else. *A Fable* is abstract also in its distance from a lived historical contingency. Faulkner appears to lack the imaginative intimacy

3. The quoted phrase is from *Selected Letters,* 348. Other letters in which Faulkner expresses a similar feeling may be found on pages 213, 314, and 378.

4. Abstraction is by no means an entirely negative trait in Faulkner's work, I should point out. For a full discussion of the matter, see Panthea Reid Broughton, *William Faulkner: The Abstract and the Actual* (Baton Rouge, La. 1974).

5. In response to a question about this at the University of Virginia, Faulkner claimed that "whenever my imagination and the bounds of that pattern conflicted, it was the pattern that bulged" (*FU* 51–52). Given the unwieldiness of the narrative, this claim can easily be believed, but even so Faulkner tacitly admits during the interchange that *A Fable* is unique in having been begun with such a pattern foremost in mind.

with his material which allows him to see the represented moment's imbrication in moments past and to come. Certainly the novel is written from above the events and outside them, as if their meaning were never immanent but only illustrative of an abstract conceptual schema. Both in the attempt to flesh out a given pattern and in the absence of historical depth, the hand of Faulkner designing in the suspect manner of Thomas Sutpen is all too evident.

Faulkner's alternative tack in these years directly opposes the strategy of *A Fable*. He insists upon the importance of historical understanding and treats any and all fixed patterns with suspicion, especially those that purport to be conclusive. More positively, he seeks a literary form which will allow for the inclusion of all other forms and all other acts of making and using fictions. His strategy, in other words, is meta-fictional. The meta-fiction he arrives upon is closely related to formal elegy, though as we shall see it is not really a literary form in a structural or generic sense. It is not, that is, a design of the sort pursued by the characters in *Absalom, Absalom!* or brandished by Faulkner in *A Fable,* a supreme fiction that might command belief or even practical application.

Snopes, Go Down, Moses, Requiem for a Nun, and to a lesser degree *The Reivers* are all informed by much the same elegiac spirit. Moreover, in all but *The Reivers,* the elegiac response to human fiction-making is elicited from stories which cover a long span of time and in so doing allow the rise and fall of particular cultural patterns to be fully depicted. *Requiem for a Nun* and *Go Down, Moses* do this by the well-practiced method of juxtaposing and counterpointing separate stories and distinct blocks of material.[6] In the three volumes of *Snopes (The Hamlet,* 1940; *The Town,*

6. This method has been commented on by several critics. Cf. Michael Millgate, *The Achievement of William Faulkner* (New York, 1971), 287 and passim.

1957; and *The Mansion,* 1959), however, Faulkner seeks a more continuous representation of historical change, and it is thus in these texts that his meta-fictional strategy is most extensively developed.

The simplest and most straightforward of the trilogy's volumes is *The Town,* and we can thus most readily observe in it the issues for which elegy eventually supplies a response and an encompassing meta-fiction. The Jefferson of that novel is a community in transition. What is at stake in the passage are the public forms and institutions which codify human relationships. Among these are the kinship patterns of the Snopeses and Stevenses, the customs of marital life and of child-raising, the economic institutions epitomized by the bank, the rituals of the older gentry displayed at the Cotillion Ball and in the courtly civilities of Judge Stevens's family at dinner, and the legal and political institutions upheld by Mayor De Spain and City Attorney Gavin Stevens.

Flem Snopes rises to power in the community by using public forms for purposes that subvert the social relations they are supposed to embody and the values they are supposed to guarantee. Jefferson's social code is as intricate and as closed to outsiders as any other small town's, and Flem at first stands before it like any raw countryman, in a state of "not knowing, of never having had any chance to learn the rules and methods" (*T* 266). But he quickly discovers that public respectability is as crucial in Jefferson as horse-trading skill had been in Frenchman's Bend, and he accordingly sets about eliminating his disreputable kinfolk and acquiring the outward tokens of respectability from Memphis furniture dealers. More importantly, he learns how to use the community's standards of decorum to gain power. He gets his first foothold in Jefferson by keeping silent about his wife's officially clandestine but widely known affair with Mayor De Spain. Later he is able to dispatch Montgomery Ward Snopes as his agent against Mink Snopes by playing on a judge's moral sensitivity. Eventually, having succeeded to the presidency of the bank by manipulating both his wife's affair and everyone else's concern for his putative daughter, he again maintains the now obviously hollow forms by inscribing on Eula's tombstone pious sentiments about her wifely virtue.

Jefferson's institutions are also being challenged by other forces. Though "nothing had happened in it, since the last carpetbagger had given up and gone home," the older era to which Judge Stevens belongs is already passing when De Spain is elected mayor (*T* 10). "It was a landslide because more than just he had won. . . . The new age had entered Jefferson" (*T* 12). Between the modernization inaugurated with De Spain and the threat that Flem is then just beginning to mount, the town is faced with deciding which of its established forms to preserve and which to alter. Most importantly, it must decide what to pass on to the new generation, whose chief exemplar is Charles Mallison. (His narrative, avowedly a representation of what the town thought in the days before he was born and while he was growing up, is precisely a record of what has been transmitted.) The awkwardness of this transition and of its confused transmission of codes from one age to the next is figuratively the town's adolescence. Seven or eight of the novel's chief characters are, in fact, either literally adolescents or explicitly described as behaving in adolescent ways.

The writer's first task with respect to the forms and institutions at issue in the community is not to find a literary form that will uphold one or another set of them but to represent the process by which they are transformed and transmitted. The solution adopted here is to make the life of the community virtually equivalent to the stories its representatives—Charles, Gavin, and Ratliff—tell about it. Most of these stories parade their status as narrative. They do not, that is, purport to be primary representations, but rather the

retelling of events which have happened and been told before. The life of the community is thus not only the events
that happen within it but the preservation or transformation
of them in stories and the narrative transmission of the
town's values to the next generation.

Faulkner himself is retelling old stories. In *The Town* he
retells (and modifies) several episodes from *The Hamlet*. In
The Mansion he retells stories from both earlier volumes and
also conducts a general roundup of his Yoknapatawpha
characters. Even in *The Hamlet,* which is otherwise firmly
established as an origin for the historical course which
ensues, Faulkner is retelling a number of short stories he had
published in the 1930s. In a sense, the entire trilogy retells a
story Faulkner had already conceived in detail and begun a
manuscript about before he had written *The Sound and the
Fury.*[7] In resonance with his tracing of Flem Snopes's career
and of the "career" of Yoknapatawpha County's social
structures, Faulkner is thus recapitulating his entire career as
a fiction writer. The concept of career as the possibility for
disciplined perpetuation and transformation accordingly becomes a major theme in the trilogy. Faulkner's writing career and the historical career of his fictional county are represented as one in these novels, for both turn on the struggle
to perpetuate, alter, and revitalize already created fictions.

The Hamlet appears some twelve years after Faulkner began work on the Snopes story. This delay and the even
longer one before the writing of the later volumes actually
enhances the importance of the trilogy to Faulkner's career.
In setting out in the late 1930s to redesign old material and
then again in the 1950s to redesign it twice more, in volumes that appear seventeen and nineteen years after *The
Hamlet,* Faulkner finds himself staking the past output of his

7. For a description of the relevant documents, see Millgate, 180–183,
and Joseph Blotner, *Faulkner: A Biography* (New York 1974), I, 526–529,
596–597.

career against its future continuation. Such risking of the past against the future is a crucial part of the trilogy's enabling principles. These, in fact, can be more particularly described as three interrelated beginning conditions and a wager upon each. The first is the existence in manuscript and in published materials of a body of already written work. Faulkner wagers that he can rewrite this material so as to make something significantly new of it. Hence the prefactory note to *The Mansion,* in which he defends the discrepancies between old and new versions of the same stories: "Since the author likes to believe, hopes that his entire life's work is a part of living literature, and since 'living' is motion, and 'motion' is change and alteration and therefore the only alternative to motion is un-motion, stasis, death, there will be found discrepancies and contradictions in the thirty-four-year progress of this particular chronicle." Not consistency or univocity but change and plurality is what must be expected in the transmission of old material.

The second enabling condition is the historical distance which Faulkner has on the events of *The Hamlet.* It allows him to narrate them more or less omnisciently. The *Hamlet* begins, in fact, at what for its inhabitants is the beginning of history. What has gone before has been forgotten or remains only as dim and barely relevant legend, like the story of the Old Frenchman. But the subsequent course of events will bring these people fully into twentieth-century world history. Faulkner's wager is that he can outwrite history itself by incorporating into his chronicle a historical understanding of events that in 1940 have not yet happened. This in turn gambles that he will find a narrative point of view which can represent events almost contemporary with some future time of writing. From the beginning, then, Faulkner requires a perspective that can supplant the initial historical omniscience. To write *The Mansion* as the contemporary episode in a long historical drama will necessitate going beyond history without leaving it behind.

The third enabling condition links the writer's particularly literary project with the tasks of his characters. Their actions are represented in the trilogy by means of a number of heterogenous literary forms and genres: Southwestern humor, chivalric romance, pastoral idyll, Greek mythology, domestic tragedy, revenge tragedy, and the historical novel. At first these several literary forms are only collected and juxtaposed, according to Faulkner's counterpoint method, which neither in principle nor by the earlier practice of *The Wild Palms* or *The Sound and the Fury* requires closure. But Faulkner's wager over the three sprawling volumes is that he can engender a meta-form which will be able to pull all these discrete forms together. Similarly, he asks of his characters at the end to respond to the entire course of events and to the vicissitudes of all the cultural forms they have seen rise and fall.

The absence of a significant past prior to the time in the 1890s at which *The Hamlet* opens is something of a necessary deception, which allows Faulkner to show a society at the birth of history. This birth, signaled by Ab Snopes's gimpy-legged stomp into Will Varner's store, marks the passage from a kind of mythic time—in which there is thought to have long been no alteration in the culture, only the repetition of traditional forms of behavior—to a fully historical time in which these traditions first become subject to change. The earlier time is mythic both for its being preserved in the legends and tales told by the men at Varner's and for the ease with which we as readers can suspect its truth. Faulkner requires, for example, that Frenchman's Bend seem an exceptionally fixed and traditional pastoral realm even though it has been settled only for about thirty years.

Like other pastorals, *The Hamlet* depicts a kind of minimal culture. Its values are embodied in just three relatively simple forms of exchange: love, trade, and narrative. Within the male society which believes it dominates the region, the two most important of these are clearly the swapping of horses and stories. Trading is the quintessential male pastime, and the shrewd trader is the figure who commands the society's greatest respect. Mink Snopes, in *The Mansion* the last relic of this world, will tell his lawyer: "You're young and eager, but that wasn't what I needed. I needed a trader, a smart trader, that knowed how to swap" (*M* 45).

One of Ratliff's stories, a version of Faulkner's earlier "Fool About a Horse," establishes at the outset the myth by which the male society believes it lives. Trading horses appears in the tale as the primary ritual of a unified and essentially harmonious culture. Its function is not exclusively economic, in the restricted sense of an exchange of commodities, but broadly social. Although the object is to win, profit is not as important as honor. "And Ab wasn't trying to beat Pat bad. He just wanted to recover that eight dollars' worth of the honor and pride of Yoknapatawpha County horse-trading, doing it not for profit but for honor" (*H* 41). A man gains simply for participating in the ritual; he need not come out on top. Ab Snopes's prestige is heightened just because he dares to challenge the legendary Pat Stamper. Trading horses serves here as a ceremonial affirmation of the society. Like a Kwakiutl potlatch, it celebrates and even helps to constitute the forms of relationship between the participants.[8] In an economy of isolated family and tenant farms, it is in fact a principal means by which unrelated men can establish social relations.

In Frenchman's Bend the ceremony of telling a story is at

8. See Marcel Mauss's classic account of the transeconomic function of exchanges like the potlatch in *The Gift,* Ian Cunnison, trans. (Glencoe, Ill. 1954), especially 31–43.

least as significant as the horse-trading ritual Ratliff tells stories about, and it more obviously goes beyond the economic domain. Sitting around Varner's porch swapping stories is a social form as important as any trading of material goods. The two are in fact functionally equivalent, for they affirm the same cultural values. In both kinds of exchange every man—teller and listener, buyer and seller—is assumed to be autonomous, worthy, and in possession of an essential dignity. The affection and mutual respect of such free and independent men for one another is apparent in their goodnatured banter and the witty strategems of sharp dealing.

The name of the myth is humor. Faulkner carefully discriminates characters who fully belong to the society—Varner, Ratliff, Bookwright—from those such as Labove, Mink, and Houston who do not possess humor. Indeed, Ratliff's story about Ab Snopes is purportedly an account of why he "soured" (*H* 33). That is, it is supposed to explain why he lost his humor and thus fell away from the community and became the barn-burning threat which all Frenchman's Bend now perceives him as. The stories Ratliff and the others trade at Varner's store are, of course, derived from the frontier humor of the Southwest. The word "humor" in fact signifies several interrelated things. There is first the literary form, as used both by Ratliff and directly by the third-person narrator. There are also the specific rituals and patterns of behavior which the stories celebrate. Finally there are the bonds that such rituals establish and the values they are meant to manifest. These values can collectively be described simply enough as the "good humor" that all men are normally supposed to possess.

Set against the humorous world as an alternative and something of a threat to it is the female world, whose chief domains are the erotic and the domestic. Mrs. Littlejohn, champion of no-nonsense domestic virtues and defender of

Ike Snopes's romance with a cow, serves as the female counterpart to Ratliff, the champion of shrewd trading and male gossip. To all the men but Ike, females are alien creatures. Even Ratliff considers them "the mortal natural enemy of the masculine race" (*H* 171). A man's relationships with women have to do primarily with maintaining self-respect before his male peers. Thus Eula Varner's suitors are often more concerned about what other men will think than about pursuing Eula. They engage in ritual combat among themselves after leaving her house, two of them flee in a desperate bid for glory when she becomes pregnant, and Labove hopes that her brother will shoot him and thus afford illusory "proof in the eyes and beliefs of living men" of his prowess as a seducer (*H* 141) Again, Ike is the only exception. His passion is the object of derisive barnyard ribaldry from the men who witness it.

According to the male myth, women are to be dominated casually but assuredly. The "Rabelaisian" Will Varner is a telling figure here, as he dispenses smoking-room stories, carries on nonchalant affairs with tenants' wives for whom he can't be bothered to remove his hat during intercourse, and maintains considerable independence from his wife and children (*H* 6). Casual dominance need not mean exploitation or subjugation. Will and his wife get along fine; so do Ab Snopes and his first wife in Ratliff's story. A man doesn't win prestige for cruelty to his wife, but he may well lose it for allowing her to interfere with his male prerogatives. In the humorous world, though Ab duly ignores his wife's complaint that he is neglecting essential domestic chores in favor of "bragging and lying to a passel of shiftless men," he shows considerable affection for her (*H* 36). Ab's loss of the cow and the mule is a major setback for a one-bale sharecropper; the situation is fully as serious as the later one that gives rise to the Armstids' tragedy. But all conflict is smiled away—so Ratliff tells it—by Ab's sympathy for the pleasure his wife gets out of a new milk separator for which they must now borrow milk.

In spite of the humorous myth, however, the relationships of men and women are more often a matter of subservience or cruel subjugation than casual dominance. The henpecked Tull is really "but the eldest daughter" of his wife (*H* 10). Mink Snopes tries to dominate his wife with threats of violence and to tie her down with the burden of a family. Yet he can never feel confident of his sexual hegemony over her, because he cannot forget her past as a "lord of the harem," commanding the logging-camp inmates to gratify her (*H* 272). Jack Houston haughtily accepts the "proferred slavedom" of women until he discovers with Lucy Pate "that until now he had not known what true slavery was—that single constant despotic undeviating will of the enslaved not only for possession, complete assimilation, but to coerce and reshape the enslaver into the seemliness of his victimization" (*H* 237). After fleeing the community and remaining away for twelve years out of fear of Lucy's silent pursuit of him, he returns at last to marry her, but buys a stallion as a reminder of his formerly "polygamous and bitless masculinity" (*H* 246). When the horse panics and kills her, then he is truly enslaved, by the twin fetters of guilt and grief.

Eula Varner is the character who most gives the lie to the men's myth of casual dominance and to their belief that sexual passion is nothing more than casual recreation. Although she is only dimly aware of her powers and does nothing to direct them, simply by her presence she dominates all the men about her. Labove, her first victim, exemplifies the enslaving nature of the desire she arouses. He realizes himself that he has been driven mad with desire, and he reacts by hating his own passion, likening it to a gangrened hand he wants to chop off. Labove is the most extreme instance of the sadomasochism which passion breeds in the men of Frenchman's Bend. Passion for him is a struggle to the death. "Fight it. Fight it. That's what it is: a man and a woman fighting each other. The hating. To kill, only to do it in such away that the other will have to know forever afterward he or she is dead" (*H* 138).

Labove teaches school and is thus excluded from the male society by profession. Moreover, he is pointedly described as a man with "humorless eyes" (*H* 125). When Eula calls him an "Ichabod Crane," she unwittingly places his story within a potentially humorous literary context and perhaps mitigates the force with which his experiences challenge the male myth (*H* 138). Yet Greek mythology, the context Labove himself invokes, seems closer to the mark. As a version of a pagan goddess, "at once supremely unchaste and inviolable," Eula reverses the myth of male dominance, for she inspires an uncontrollable passion in men to whose advances she remains indifferent (*H* 131).

Even Hoake McCarron's deflowering of Eula represents a defeat for the men of Frenchman's Bend. No local suitor is man enough for her. The swaggering Hoake is no master of the situation either. It is Eula who, according to rumor, has vanquished three of the five suitors who ambush the couple; it is she who must contrive to support his broken arm when she finally gives herself to him.

Eula is at several points in the novel linked to the natural fecundity of earth, most notably by Labove in accurately prophesying her husband's impotence.

[He] would not possess her but merely own her by the single strength which power gave, the dead power of money, wealth, gewgaws, baubles, as he might own, not a picture, statue: a field, say. He saw it: the fine land rich and fecund and foul and eternal and impervious to him who claimed title to it, oblivious, drawing to itself tenfold the quantity of living seed its owner's whole life could have secreted and compounded, producing a thousandfold the harvest he could ever hope to gather and save. [*H* 135]

The myth requires that working the land allow one the leisure for more essential pursuits like gossip and barter. But to take the traditional association of land and women seriously is to realize that the men are no more masters of the land than they are of Eula. The humorless among them understand just that.

> There now remained the small neat farm which likewise had been worked to the point of mute and unflagging mutual hatred and resistance but which could not leave him and so far had not been able to eject him but which possibly knew that it could and would outlast him. . . . At home there was that work waiting, the constant and unflagging round of repetitive nerve-and-flesh wearing labor by which alone that piece of earth which was his mortal enemy could fight him with, which he had performed yesterday and must perform again today and again tomorrow and tomorrow. [H 219]

Land and women are both enemies to the male society, challenging the humorous myth and the possibility of good humor about life in Frenchman's Bend.

Whereas Eula represents a challenge from without, Flem mounts a parasitic challenge to the male society from within. His early career, before anyone quite comprehends the threat he represents, is often an unwitting parody of the trading ritual, a taking of the letter for the spirit. He is an object of amazed comedy to the narrator and to the community in his initial attempts to imitate Will Varner. He is not another Will Varner but only his "parrot-taught headman," manipulating forms whose import escapes him (H 69). If his white shirt and machine-made bow tie are proleptic images of his depthless and mechanical soul, they are also, to the amusement of his overall-clad observers, a pathetically premature uniform of middle-class status.

At every point Flem insists on the letter of the law and the fine print on the contract, usually at the expense of the more liberal values of the other traders. Occasionally this punctiliousness is to his embarrassment, as when he refuses to grant credit to anyone at the store and must be reprimanded by Will, and even to his financial disadvantage, as when he replaces Jody's profitable carelessness about making change with infallible accuracy. More often, however, his precision is essential to his success, as Ratliff acknowledges when he imagines Flem relying on *"what the banking and the civil laws states in black and white"* to best the Prince of Hell (*H* 172).

Unlike his father in the old days, Flem never places honor and prestige above profit. He perverts the trading ritual by making it narrowly economic, denying the social bonds it is meant to create. Even the triumph of the victorious trader establishes a kind of human relationship, but Flem never boasts of his deals or attempts to elicit admiration for his crafty methods. Years later no one knows for certain if he was the owner of the spotted horses. The ritual calls for face-to-face dealings, but Flem works in secrecy. It is licit for Pat Stamper to outwit you and even to cheat you, but he must do it right there in front of you and thus acknowledge your existence. Flem, however, customarily works through intermediaries like Buck Hipps, Lump Snopes, and Eustace Grimm, thus denying the affirmations of relatedness and mutual status which the ritual is supposed to constitute.

In reaction to early interpretations of Flem's career, which saw in it an allegorical battle between his malignant modernity and the older, more humane ways of first Frenchman's Bend and then Jefferson, Joseph Gold has argued persuasively that Flem and his cohorts are fundamentally no different from the community they invade.[9] One could thus argue

9. Joseph Gold, "The Normality' of Snopesism," *Wisconsin Studies in Contemporary Literature* (now *Contemporary Literature*), 3 (Winter 1962), 25–34.

that Flem does little more than make manifest the harsh economic underpinnings of a barter society in a land of great poverty. Trade is economic competition, after all, and invariably produces winners and losers. Will Varner is a "usurer" and is popularly believed to spend his hours in the barrel chair planning his next mortgage foreclosure (*H* 5). Even Ratliff is "not to be denied" as he collects his debts months before the harvest will bring any spare cash into the hands of his customers (*H* 63). Moreover, Flem's dealings are far from the only episodes in which we see the envy and greed that economic competition can engender. The dispute between Mink and Houston ends in murder. The old farmer who retrieves Houston's cow and the soured Ab Snopes share a bitter resentment of their fate as poor whites.

The myth of the male society is not simply a pretty fiction designed to cover up a greedily acquisitive society, however. If Flem's career is in some ways only an exposure of the true character of the local economy, his inhumanity and his indifference to anything but profit are nonetheless significant matters. Flem's villainy lies not in outsmarting the community by selling the men useless and uncatchable horses but in his willingness to ruin the Armstids for a five-dollar sale. Like a caricature of economic man as described by Adam Smith and condemned by Karl Marx, Flem turns every good into a commodity and makes every value a monetary one. This is not so true of the other traders, even those who have every intention of making a profit. Buck Hipps tries to return Mrs. Armstid's money. Ratliff gives away the profits of his goat deal. And in *The Mansion* we are told that Will Varner has tried to pay the pound fee which so aggravates Mink Snopes.

At issue here is the relation of a society's fictions to its actual behavior. To deem as the basic realities of the culture the enslavements which men can suffer to passion or greed and thus to see the humorous myth as only a palliative fiction is to endorse what has been called the "environmental theory" of Southwestern humor.[10] Conditions on the frontier or in Frenchman's Bend are so terrible that a humorous fantasy must be created to make life bearable. Humor is the specific candidate for such a fantasy in *The Hamlet,* but in *Snopes* as a whole Faulkner extends the question to all social and cultural forms. Do any of them really establish humane values, or are they all either cloaks for exploitation and brutality or empty fictions that carry no value or force in themselves?

In *The Hamlet* the burden of these questions falls chiefly on Ratliff, and the problem is made to be simultaneously a matter of literary and cultural history. Ratliff's two stories at the opening of the novel establish him as the humorous conscience of the community and also as the obvious descendant of a number of nineteenth-century American literary figures. His command of the vernacular and his usual clear-sightedness reveal him as particularly indebted to George Washington Harris's Sut Luvingood and Twain's Huck Finn.[11] In earlier stories—"A Bear Hunt," "Lizards in Jamshyd's Courtyard," "Spotted Horses," and *Sartoris/Flags in the Dust*—Ratliff (originally called Suratt) is even more directly a descendant of Sut and Huck. But in *The Hamlet* there is one important difference: Ratliff is not himself normally an object of comedy. Although both Twain and Harris, unlike many other writers of frontier humor, were deeply committed to most of the values expressed by their unsophisticated heroes, both were capable of exploiting the lack of sophistication to win a laugh. Faulkner, however, allows Ratliff a native shrewdness which discourages the reader from feeling superior to him.

10. For a summary of this theory and an annotated bibliography of its leading proponents and critics, see John Q. Anderson, "Scholarship in Southwestern Humor—Past and Present," *Mississippi Quarterly,* 17 (Spring 1964), 67–86.

11. Faulkner has included Sut Luvingood, who is not always noted for the quality of his insight, among his favorite literary figures for the specific reason that Sut has "no illusions about himself" (*LG* 251).

Ratliff possesses humor both in the sense of a faculty for perceiving and relating comic incongruities and also in the sense of good humor, a healthy temperament or a "moral, spiritual eupepsia" as Faulkner once called it (*FU* 253). However, Faulkner's obvious fondness for Ratliff, whom he has named along with Dilsey as the favorites among his own characters, and the rather sentimental portrayal of him in *The Mansion* should not blind us to the ways his humor is tested in *The Hamlet* (*LG* 224). The virtues of humor and some of the weaknesses which the encounters with Flem, Eula, and Ike will demonstrate as ensuing from these virtues are suggested by the epithets repeatedly attached to Ratliff. He is "shrewd," possessing a practical intelligence rather than the more speculative mind of Gavin Stevens. He is "affable," friendly and sociable, but always on a purely conversational level, as the word's etymology suggests. The deeper attachments which, for example, Ike feels for his cow or Eula inspires in Labove are alien to him. He is also "bland" and "impenetrable," preserving both his equanimity and his distance and treasuring a kind of reserve that allows him to feel quietly superior to men who can be tricked into buying wild ponies.[12]

12. The weaknesses of Ratliff's humorous outlook are not fully revealed until the last book of *The Hamlet* unless we read significance, as I think we ought to, into the differences between the original version of "Barn Burning" and Ratliff's retelling. (The original may be found in the June 1939 issue of *Harper's*, pages 89–96, and, slightly revised, in Faulkner's 1950 *Collected Stories*. That both Faulkner and his publishers considered Ratliff's a substantively different story is indicated by the failure to include it among the frontispiece acknowledgments of other previously published stories used in the novel.) The short story is a moving and quite tragic piece centering on the almost Satanic figure of Ab and on his youngest son's struggle between filial loyalty and a sense of right and wrong. Ratliff reduces the cold malice of Ab and eliminates the son's perspective by means of a joke which the short story reveals to be unwittingly callous: "There was another one, too, a little one. . . . Maybe they forgot to tell him when to get outen the barn" (*H* 15). As in his response to Eula's marriage, his reaction to Ike's romance, and his comments in

Eula and Ike challenge Ratliff's good humor by posing a positive alternative to it. Sexual passion is an implicit threat to his customary balance and moderation. During his uncharacteristic and far from good-humored self-laceration about his motives in taking Ike's beloved cow away, he seems to admit to Mrs. Littlejohn that love might have its claims which he cannot understand. Later, reflecting on Eula's marriage to Flem, he acknowledges that "that would never have been for him, not even at the prime summer peak of what he and Varner both would have called his tomcatting's heyday" (*H* 182).

Ratliff's horror at Ike's mere existence is a more direct threat to humor, since Ike's idiocy represents not simply something he cannot share but something he cannot accept. "I don't know as I would believe that [Ike was made in God's image] even if I knowed it was true" (*H* 93). Ratliff sees in the idiot "the eyes which at some instant, some second once, had opened upon, been vouchsafed a glimpse of, the Gorgon-face of that primal injustice which man was not intended to look at face to face" (*H* 98). Against such a vision Ratliff's belief in the basic decency of life is completely helpless. He has begun to discover encroaching upon his humorous outlook a far more grotesque comedy which discerns at the heart of things a "prime maniacal Risibility" that makes jokes on humanity, not for it (*H* 215).[13]

The only responses to Ike Snopes which Ratliff can summon are, as he recognizes, inadequate to the preservation of humor. "Thank God men have done learned how to forget quick what they aint brave enough to try to cure" (*H* 99). In response to Flem's rapacity, however, which also soon ap-

---

The Town after Eula's suicide, Ratliff's humor is either blind or indifferent to the extremities of passion and tragedy.

13. Cf. Alan Howard, "Huck Finn in the House of Usher: The Comic and Grotesque Worlds of *The Hamlet*," *Southern Review* (Adelaide, Australia), 5 (1972), 125–146.

pears to Ratliff as something which just shouldn't exist, Ratliff fights to restore the humorous world by trying to subdue Flem to its forms. Ratliff's first plan, the intricate and at best only marginally profitable goat-trading deal, is useful to him precisely because it employs the humorous riposte of setting the barn-burning propensities of the Snopes clan against a Snopes. But because of Flem's willingness to exploit Ike's idiocy, Ratliff is unable to keep the trade within the ceremonial forms of humor. Even though his plan otherwise succeeds, Ratliff emerges from the deal emotionally devastated.

Ratliff's attitude toward Flem and the other Snopeses becomes increasingly one of despair, as the claims of humor seem more and more betrayed by Flem's success. Despair is the chief sign of failure for all the characters in the trilogy who are trying to maintain old forms and values against the various forces which challenge them. We see its effects on Gavin Stevens in *The Town,* and we see Mink Snopes's lonely, successful struggle against it in *The Mansion.* Despair is defined rather precisely in *Snopes* as a loss of faith in the power of forms to preserve humane values, a loss of faith which quickly extends to the possibility of maintaining those values by any means. In *The Hamlet* it is also linked to the failure of articulate expression. Despair's advance is signaled by the cries of inarticulate horror voiced by the Prince of Hell, by the judge in Tull's lawsuit, and by Ratliff himself (*H* 175, 380, 367).

Ratliff initially can imagine Jody's horror at being "passed" by Flem as a yet humorous because well-deserved comeuppance (*H* 68). Even the much grimmer parable of Flem in hell is still recognizably a frontier tall tale. But Ratliff's malicious (and unfounded) story of Flem seducing a black customer and his spasmodic parody of I.O. Snopes's proverbs are the last resources of a man on the brink of losing his sense of humor. The climax of Ratliff's growing despair begins with the "terror" in his eyes as he observes St. Elmo Snopes, the goatlike epitome of pure Snopes rapacity (*H* 365). Later that afternoon, after he realizes how callously Flem has exploited the Armstids, his explanation of why he hasn't himself reimbursed Mrs. Armstid (as he had earlier reimbursed Ike) turns into a desperate protest against both the Snopeses and their willing victims.

> I wasn't protecting a Snopes [i.e., Ike] from Snopeses; I wasn't even protecting a people from a Snopes. I was protecting something that wasn't even a people, that wasn't nothing but something that dont want nothing but to walk and feel the sun and wouldn't know how to hurt no man even if it would and wouldn't want to even if it could, just like I wouldn't stand by and see you steal a meat-bone from a dog. I never made them Snopses and I never made the folks that cant wait to bare their backsides to them. I could do more, but I wont. I wont, I tell you! [*H* 367]

Ratliff now realizes in anguish that Flem's success is a direct function of the community's willingness to let its worst aspects come to the fore. The viciousness, greed, and cruelty Flem can manipulate in Henry Armstid now live within the once humorous community and can no longer be considered alien evils which the outsider Flem uses against it. Yet Ratliff still implicitly excludes himself from among those who allow themselves to be exploited, just as earlier he had assumed that greed and cruelty were limited to the Snopeses and served to exclude them from the community. Ratliff has been willing to admit that he might be a "pharisee" about the claims of passion (*H* 227). But most of his behavior in the novel, while not exactly self-righteous, has been predicated on his own immunity to the lures by which Flem has prospered in Frenchman's Bend.

The immunity proves nonexistent when Ratliff succumbs to the lure of the Old Frenchman's treasure. " 'A salted gold mine,' Uncle Gavin said. 'One of the oldest tricks in the world, yet you fell for it. Not Henry Armstid: you' " (*T* 8). The ruined splendor of the Old Frenchman's place is a patent symbol of the vanity of human wishes, a vanity to which Ratliff now shows himself vulnerable. He, Bookwright, and Armstid are represented as raping the earth when they dig for treasure; Ratliff's greed becomes so feverish that he wrestles with Bookwright over possession of a shovel to dig with. But Ratliff finally realizes what he is doing and with this realization salvages a remnant of his humor. "God, . . . look at what even the money a man aint got yet will do to him" (*H* 393). He draws back in time to be able to laugh at his own gullibility and to make a comically self-deprecating wager with Bookwright about the dates on the planted coins. Armstid, in contrast, remains in the throes of greed and soon goes mad.

Ratliff's recovery of his humor is a victory of sorts over the advance of Snopesism. He can now acknowledge that he too is capable of greed and cruelty but that these qualities are not something to which he must be enslaved. The perversion of the community's fictions does not quite mean the disappearance of the values they once seemed to uphold. Yet the victory is limited to Ratliff himself and to Bookwright, who serves throughout as Ratliff's Ratliff. The others have either been corrupted—like Will Varner, who "looks like he is fixing to snopes forever" (*H* 185)—or stand helpless before Flem's expropriation of their cultural forms, like the crowd which stands around Henry Armstid at the end of the novel.

Nevertheless, the limited countermovement represented by Ratliff's recovery of his humor foreshadows the strategy Faulkner seeks in the trilogy as a whole. Humor, divorced from the specific literary and cultural forms to which it was attached at the beginning and standing alone and insubstantial as a personal assertion of value is the trilogy's first broaching of a meta-fiction. It is not, in fact, really a meta-fiction because it is not specifically concerned with human fiction-making, but it shares with the later elegiac vision the characteristic of being a value-standing attitude which is not embodied in a specific form. Faulkner continues to insert humorous stories into subsequent volumes ("Mule in the Yard" or "By the People"), and until the very end Ratliff maintains his humorous attitude toward Snopesism. Humor *per se* is not the central issue in *The Town* and *The Mansion,* however. Rather, what is at stake there are the values attached to the more institutionalized forms of Jefferson's civic life.

The movement in *The Hamlet* toward discrediting social institutions and cultural forms completes itself in *The Town* and *The Mansion,* and it does so in a fashion explicit enough to make a lengthy analysis superflous. Established forms of human interaction are exposed as both empty and all-powerful. On the one hand, Flem succeeds in taking control of Jefferson's civic institutions and perverting the values they were meant to secure. His chief opponent, Gavin Stevens, a defender of the established forms of honor and propriety for their own sake, finds that a stand in favor of such forms usually works to Flem's advantage. The law Gavin upholds as an officer of the courts and the genteel customs he desperately clings to serve not as bulwarks against Flem's advance but as structures which Flem can easily manipulate for his own ends. On the other hand, however, when Flem reaches his pinnacle and has fully consolidated his control over these structures, he finds that he possesses nothing of real value to him. Instead he is entombed by the very structures he has struggled so long to appropriate.

Gavin Stevens is patently a quixotic figure, especially in *The Town.* He makes continual recourse to "poets' dreams" as the source of his values and of his faith in established forms, but he is frequently willing to help compromise his own ideals rather than to see their formal embodiments fall entirely (*T* 226). Thus he fights a gallantly absurd duel with De Spain over the "principle that chastity and virtue in women shall be defended whether they exist or not" (*T* 76). More important, his defense of established forms makes him Flem's accomplice in several of the latter's most crucial stratagems: obtaining entry into Jefferson society, railroading Montgomery Ward Snopes to the penitentiary, and arranging a church burial for the suicide Eula.

Gavin's attempt to oppose himself to Flem by upholding forms that even he eventually begins to realize are hollow dramatizes the secret complicity between the two. Both men depend on established codes, and both are willing to impose them on others. Much of the battle between the two is waged over Eula and Linda, and both men try in different ways to coerce the women into acting in public according to codes the men determine. (Whereas in *The Hamlet* the female society offers an alternative set of social forms—domestic and sexual—in *The Town* and *The Mansion* women rather unpersuasively are meant to represent mysterious natural forces who are beyond the need for forms. Faulkner's conception of life as motion becomes an explicit doctrine in these volumes. Women, especially Eula Varner Snopes, are the primary representatives of a vital motion for which men seek appropriate forms of arrest. Not only is such a conception obviously sexist, it works against the requirements of the narrative. Faulkner's recurrent misogyny produces brilliant writing in *As I Lay Dying, Light in August,* and *The Wild Palms;* however, in much of *The Town* and in the sections of *The Mansion* dealing with Linda Snopes he seems unable to supply the imaginative complexity demanded by the importance he ascribes to his female characters.)

Both the emptiness of official structures of human interchange and their imprisoning power are represented by Flem's situation in *The Mansion*. President of the bank, owner of an antebellum mansion, and nominally the most powerful man in Yoknapatawpha County, Flem is "completely complete" (*M* 154). But he has sacrificed to those public forms whatever capacity he may ever have had to enjoy them. "When he had nothing, he could afford to chew tobacco; when he had a little, he could afford to chew gum; when he found out he could be rich provided he just didn't die beforehand, he couldn't afford to chew anything" (*M* 66). We see him always "chewing steady on nothing"; along with his sexual impotence, the "little chunk of Frenchman's Bend air" on which his jaws continually work becomes the image for the emptiness at the center of his official control over the community's institutions (*M* 157).

In part we can assimilate Flem to the many other fictional characters who have given over the direction of their own desire to others. "*He had sacrificed everything . . . to gain the only prize he knew since it was the only one he could understand since the world itself as he understood it assured him that was what he wanted because that was the only thing worth having*" (*M* 240). Official forms and established institutions play the role of the mediator for Flem in the operation of what René Girard has called triangular desire; like the characters Girard analyzes, Flem discovers the desired object, the mansion, to be his "mausoleum" (*M* 359).[14] Once he has attained the goals defined by others, he becomes incapable of answering the question Montgomery Ward poses: "Jesus, you do want to stay alive, don't you. Only, why?" (*M* 70).

Ratliff in *The Hamlet* and Gavin in *The Town* despair at the powerlessness of forms to preserve human values, at their inability to secure positive human relationships. The dark vision now becomes the discovery that such forms by themselves carry no values and establish no relationships at all. Flem's isolation and emptiness are duplicated in *The*

14. René Girard, *Deceit, Desire, and the Novel*, Yvonne Freccero, trans. (Baltimore 1965).

Mansion by the experience of his putative daughter Linda, whose dependence on organized structures links Faulkner's theme to wider currents of twentieth-century history. Faulkner presents her membership in the Communist party, her patriotic work in the war against Hitler, and her well-meaning but abstractly motivated civil rights work as memorials to her dead husband and ineffective replacements for their marriage. She becomes in her deafness someone who lives "outside human time," a Keatsian "bride of quietude and silence striding inviolate in the isolation of unhearing" (*M* 236, 230). Thirty years before, such a figure would have represented a desired aesthetic transcendence for Faulkner, but now it denotes a terrifying alienation from all human interchange, even, at the end, with her protector Gavin. "She just stood, our eyes almost level, looking at me out of, across, something—abyss, darkness; not abject, not questioning, not even hoping" (*M* 238).

Established forms, rather than serving as instruments of social intercourse and embodiments of humane values, prove to be the graveyard of once vital relations and values. Forms refer only to bygone value; the institutions that Flem commands are only the petrified remnants of a vitality which flourished before he took over. His antebellum mansion is the now vacant symbol of a once meaningful society. Gavin recognizes this, at least conceptually, during his one climactic moment of insight in *The Town*. "Because the tragedy of life is, it must be premature, inconclusive and inconcludable, in order to be life; it must be before itself, in advance of itself, to have been at all" (*T* 317–318). The Motion—Faulkner now begins to capitalize the word—and creative energy that genuinely establish human relationships always precede the forms in which we retrospectively see the relationships.

Like the designs in *Absalom, Absalom!*, social forms in the trilogy seem both inescapable and incapacitating. Flem and

Gavin's battle and their secret complicity is, in fact, another version of the relation between Sutpen and Quentin. Like Gavin and Quentin, we grow up in the midst of structures which appear to provide our only means of relating to others and thus we become their confused and stymied defenders. Or, like Flem and Sutpen, we appropriate them from the outside and are made over in their image. Unless we are as strong and lucky as Sutpen and can die before understanding how completely devoid of values the established forms are, we find ourselves in despair, like Gavin at the end of *The Town,* overtaken by paralysis, like Flem at the end of *The Mansion,* or suffering from both, like Quentin in *Absalom, Absalom!*

The literary counterpart to this situation is not so emphasized in *The Town* and the earlier part of *The Mansion* as in *The Hamlet;* it is nonetheless easy enough to see. Faulkner finds himself with a strong conviction about the values which ought to be manifest in human relationships. All of them are traditional humanistic values: courage, kindness, honor, and the like. But every traditional or invented literary fiction in which he attempts to represent these values turns out to be at best inadequate or incomplete and at worst an accomplice in the betrayal of those values. Frontier humor in *The Hamlet* not only proves insufficient for representing life in Frenchman's Bend, but its use by Ratliff and the others as an operative cultural myth makes them that much more defenseless against Flem Snopes. The same may be said about the dreams of Gavin Stevens's poets.

The story of Mink Snopes in *The Mansion* offers the counter to this desperate situation and the first step in the strategy by which Faulkner seeks to go beyond the constraints of determinate literary forms without abandoning the specificity of the fluid materiality they organize. By the time Mink leaves prison he has been systematically deprived of any place in the social system or any role within the culturally sanctioned forms of exchange. He is so much an anachronism in the modern world which has grown up during his imprisonment that he is rightly terrified of falling prey to laws and customs which have arisen in his absence. Now a kind of stripped integer, a man reduced to what is uniquely his own, Mink is an inverse mirror to his cousin Flem. Whereas Flem begins by exerting a sheer will to power and ends up imprisoned by having given over his will to the established forms of power, Mink, who begins as an individual firmly if unhappily placed in a network of kinship relations, economic obligations, and traditional customs, has lost the use of all these structured connections in the actual prison at Parchman and is left only with a fierce will to assert his bond with Flem.

In one respect Mink is a paragon of self-reliance, but his is not an Emersonian reliance on the self to be complete unto itself. His independence is a capacity to be able, without depending on established forms of relationship, to insist upon his relatedness to others. Mink asserts his selfhood not as a principle of autonomy but as part of a relationship to Flem. Flem's original outrage to Mink had been a violation of the "ancient immutable laws of simple blood kinship," but by the time Mink gets out of prison the recognition he intends to elicit from Flem is something different (*M* 5). It is both more primitive, since it is the fundamental recognition of mutual selfhood between persons, and also more a product of Mink's own creative effort, since it is brought fully into being only at the moment when the two men confront each other.

Mink's self-reliance is also qualified by an ambiguous and perhaps somewhat suspect religious vision, which turns on the distinction Faulkner means to establish between trust and dependence.[15] When Mink commits the murder that

15. Faulkner has used this distinction before. Joe Christmas prefers McEachern's abstract and impersonal dependability to the kindness of Mrs. McEachern, who insists on trusting Joe (*LA* 157–158).

first sends him to prison, the cold-blooded ambush of Jack
Houston, he is already very much the proud, self-reliant
loner. But he firmly believes he can depend on *"them—
they—it,* whichever and whatever you wanted to call it,
who represented a simple fundamental justice and equity in
human affairs, or else a man might just as well quit" (*M* 6).
Suffering Houston's insolence has gained him the "right to
depend on *them* which he had earned by never before in his
life demanding anything of them" (*M* 6–7).

By the time Mink leaves prison and sets off to kill Flem,
however, his dependence on *"them"* to secure justice for
him has been supplanted by a less clearly defined trust. Like
Ratliff and the others who have come from Frenchman's
Bend, he refers now to Old Moster, a figure who is for
Mink less a genuinely external force than an emanation of
Mink's own "confidence" (*M* 100). Mink's faith in Old
Moster is, in effect, a trope for his ability to go on hoping
that he will have the opportunity to depend on himself.
Mink is thus able to do successfully what Ratliff recom-
mends: "So what you need is to learn how to trust in God
without depending on Him. In fact, we need to fix things so
He can depend on us for a while" (*M* 321).

The elusive semantic margin between trusting and depending marks the difference between a personal assumption of the responsibility to create new value and a reliance
upon forms in which such value has been previously established. The distinction is crucial to the last phase of Faulkner's career, for it turns the question of the fate of designs
that always prove inadequate back upon the designer's responsibility to keep on working the design and transforming it. The same personal contribution of value can be seen
in Aunt Molly's arrangement of a funeral for her grandson
in *Go Down, Moses* and Nancy Mannigoe's actions in *Requiem for a Nun.* Here also, although the bond which Mink
creates is accomplished by a murder and the revitalized

human relationship lasts only for the brief moment of recognition between Mink and Flem (while Flem waits silently for the other to fire his pistol a second time), Mink's action is clearly a triumph. Against all odds and almost entirely from his own resources, Mink has created an authentically mutual relationship where before there had been only the empty form of distant kinship and Flem's lifelong refusal of mutuality.

The burden of Mink's actions fall on Gavin Stevens, and so more heavily does the burden of Linda's furtive complicity in the murder. Gavin is required at last to take a responsibility upon himself which violates the forms he has before so carefully and ineffectually tended. At the point where established forms seem most to have crumbled, he proves capable of envisioning a new and very different kind of human relatedness. Having seen Linda shatter the image of perfect fidelity and grief he had made of her, having seen her betray his trust in her, and having then taken responsibility for her action to the point of condoning murder and even delivering at her behest a packet of getaway money to Mink, Gavin finds that he no longer needs to defend the official institutions of Jefferson or to think in terms of abstract and idealistic moral categories.

> "There aren't any morals," Stevens said. "People just do the best they can."
> "The poor sons of bitches, " Ratliff said.
> "The poor sons of bitches," Stevens said. "Drive on. Pick it up." [*M* 429]

Gavin's phrase, "the poor sons of bitches that have to cause all the grief and anguish they have to cause" (*M* 430), climaxes a refrain which runs throughout *The Mansion*. Like Brother Goodyhay and Miss Reba, Gavin and Ratliff mean by it "all of us, everyone of us" (*M* 82). Envisioned for the first time here is a kind of fundamental human relatedness that includes all mankind, victim and victimizer alike, in a single community. It is a community of suffering and striving, the striving which Mink and for that matter Flem also exemplify and the suffering which both of them cause and endure. Human bonds within such a community arise not from the performance of prescribed functions in an established structure but from the ongoing effort of individuals continually involved in the work of transforming relationships and values. Value thus comes from the energy, the motion, that the individual puts into its creation. But as a part of Motion, the individual is already part of a universal community, from the well-nigh cosmic perspective which Gavin has begun to glimpse and which the trilogy now advances.

Faulkner moves here toward the elision of the middle term in the series that runs from the person to the society to mankind. The forms and institutions of a specific society, Frenchman's Bend or Jefferson, establish that society as a discrete unit by defining boundaries, excluding what is outside, and classifying what is inside.[16] Over against such societies and encompassing them without either contravening or supporting their specific codes, Faulkner sets a vision of community which is deliberately indefinite, inclusive, and undifferentiated. Frenchman's Bend and Jefferson, past and present, and Mink and Flem all become fundamentally indistinguishable from this perspective. All belong to the persistence of human motion and effort within a world of flux and change. The motion of life within a flux of specific cultural forms becomes, in fact, the object of Faulkner's simultaneously celebratory and melancholy vision. Both the successes and the failures of human effort to establish rela-

16. Cf. Charles Mallison's comment on Jefferson: "Ours was a town founded by Aryan Baptists and Methodists, for Aryan Baptists and Methodists . . . not to escape from tyranny as they claimed and believed, but to establish one" (*T* 306–307).

tionships and to maintain cultural forms are ultimately transitory, but the effort persists. In motion, in a refusal of stasis
and despair, are discovered the sources of a vitality that both
causes all the grief and anguish and affords a continuing
hope of supplanting them.

Faulkner's vision of mankind's endurance appears within a
definable literary context. The conclusion of *The Mansion*
rewrites the entire trilogy as an elegy, here specifically a pastoral elegy. As for Milton, Shelley, and Tennyson, elegy is
for Faulkner ultimately a celebratory genre. But the speakers
in "Lycidas," "Adonais," and "In Memoriam" must first
grieve for what has passed before they can achieve a vision of
the enduring or the eternal. Their eventually joyful vision
transforms and, in effect, repudiates the initial grief. In
Faulkner's version, however, the lamentation for what has
been lost and the celebration of what is discovered to endure
occur simultaneously. Neither response offers a higher order
of truth. By contrast to the durable conventions of elegiac
verse, in which the victory of the eternal over the temporal
and mutable is trumpeted, Faulkner insists joy and grief are
both to be found in time. Mink, Faulkner's humble counterpart to Shelley's Adonais, is not exalted as a new god or
translated into the divine spirit but interred among all those
who have been part of motion and change.

Ultimately the community to which Mink belongs is the
community of those who have been. It is into a pantheon of
the dead who have suffered and striven that Mink enters at
the close of the novel in the virtuoso passage of celebratory
prose.

> He could feel that Mink Snopes that had had to spend so much
> of his life just having unnecessary bother and trouble, begin-
> ning to creep, seep, flow easy as sleeping; he could almost
> watch it, following all the little grass blades and tiny roots, the
> little holes the worms made, down and down into the ground
> already full of the folks that had the trouble but were free now,

so that it was just the ground and the dirt that had to bother
and worry and anguish with the passions and hopes and skeers,
the justice and the injustice and the griefs. [*M* 435]

Faulknerian man becomes himself for having walked up-
right, for having taken the bother to struggle against the
seductive pull of the earth in order to create value in his life.
The pull of the earth then becomes an earned caress and the
dissolution of death a reward for his striving. It is Mink's
refusal to give up, his capacity to go on struggling for value,
that earns his place among all the others of legend and song.

All mixed and jumbled up comfortable and easy so wouldn't
nobody even know or even care who was which any more,
himself among them, equal to any, good as any, brave as any,
being inextricable from, anonymous with all of them: the beautiful, the splendid, the proud and the brave, right on up to the
very top itself among the shining phantoms and dreams which
are the milestones of the long human recording—Helen and the
bishops, the kings and the unhomed angels, the scornful and
graceless seraphim. [*M* 435–436]

These final phrases repeat the words used in *The Hamlet*
to describe the earth that Ike Snopes walks upon with his
beloved (*H* 213). Like Mink, Ike is an outcast and to the
others in Frenchman's Bend only marginally human. But on
the edge of society, away from its forms, Ike has created a
life worthy of the lushly idyllic prose Faulkner bestows
upon him. Ike's bizarre love story is the genuine pastoral
within the nominally pastoral community of Frenchman's
Bend. He has truly gone outside the culture when he steals
Houston's cow. But as the ornate and highly literary language of his story is meant to suggest, what lies outside an
established culture may be not nature but the more humane
culture Ike himself founds. It is thus the least of Faulkner's
characters in the trilogy, Mink and Ike, who are the exemplary figures for the genuinely human capability that goes

beyond the established structures of society and is ultimately the base on which those more transitory and partial forms are established.

The same understanding can be observed in most of the other novels of Faulkner's last phase: in *Requiem for a Nun* certainly, and quite baldly in the declamatory passages of *A Fable*, but also in the elegiac structure of the otherwise more somber *Go Down, Moses*. Faulkner's elegiac vision receives its fullest, most impressive expression in the final chapter of *The Mansion*, however, a chapter which looks back over the entire trilogy and transforms its meaning. The chapter looks back on Faulkner's entire career, in fact, for he has been careful to include in *The Mansion* a last retelling of stories from the whole span of his fiction and to make brief allusions to an even larger number of novels and tales. Events from books written around 1930, for example—*Sartoris/Flags in the Dust*, *The Sound and the Fury*, and *Sanctuary*—are rehearsed once more. Even relatively obscure short stories such as "Uncle Willy" and "Shingles for the Lord" are recalled.

Mink's death in the last chapter is a secular version of elegiac apotheosis. The chapter's affinity with pastoral elegy is further sustained by an insistently autumnal tone. Mink, Gavin, and Ratliff are all old men now. The Frenchman's Bend in which they meet is not the "rich river-bottom country" of *The Hamlet* (3) but a land of eroded farms awaiting the winter.

The sun had crossed the equator, in Libra now; and in the cessation of motion and the quiet of the idling engine, there was a sense of autumn after the slow drizzle of Sunday and the bright spurious cool which had lasted through Monday almost; the jagged rampart of pines and scrub oak was a thin dike against the winter and rain and cold, under which the worn-out fields overgrown with sumac and sassafras and persimmon had already turned scarlet. [M 417]

From this local autumn emerges an autumn of the cosmos and also the autumn of Faulkner's writing and of his career.

> Stevens found the fading earthen steps again, once more up and out into the air, the night, the moonless dark, the worn-out eroded fields supine beneath the first faint breath of fall, waiting for the winter. Overhead, celestial and hierarchate, the constellations wheeled through the zodiacal pastures: Scorpion and Bear and Scales; beyond cold Orion and the Sisters the fallen and homeless angels choired, lamenting. [*M* 433]

The elegiac form with which the trilogy concludes differs from the numerous other literary forms, fictions, and genres employed elsewhere in the three volumes. It both is and is not the final form of *Snopes* and a last fiction to which all the others in Faulkner's work are assimilated. It is final in the sense that it explicitly concludes the trilogy and implicitly concludes the career, thus taking upon itself all that has gone before. It is final also in that it has a kind of privileged status in relation to forms which have gone before.

Yet it is not strictly comparable to these others. Unlike them, it is not a way of arresting motion or (to paraphrase another of Faulkner's descriptions of fiction-making) a means of stopping the motion of life and holding a light up to it.[17] Elegy offers Faulkner not a determinate shaping of life but a response to the many shapings of it. In the same way that the community of mankind stands in relation to the particular social structures it encompasses, elegy stands as a meta-fiction to all fictions and fiction-making. Rather than arresting motion in some discrete social, literary, or conceptual structure, elegy as meta-fiction celebrates the existence of arrest and motion as constant forces that can never be brought together in a single, final, and total structure.

Faulkner's writing career thus concludes by demonstrat-

17. "You catch this fluidity which is human life and you focus a light on it and you stop it long enough for people to be able to see it" (*FU* 239).

ing that its task, the making of fictions and the structuring of experience, can never be concluded. In fact, Faulkner wrote one more novel before he died. *The Reivers* is like a detail from the panels in *Go Down, Moses* or the mural in *Snopes*. It represents a boy's coming of age as the comic conflict between the designs inherited from his parents and those of his own which he is trying to establish for the first time. The comedy ends by showing these designs as fundamentally compatible, this being the structural counterpart to the comic tone, and by presenting itself as the boy's narration many years later to his own grandson. The process goes on; designs are established and then passed on as narratives to be adopted, transformed, or rejected by those who come after.

To say this in another way, Faulkner's career does not come to a point of closure or fasten upon some conclusive program which would designate finite boundaries for his work. He creates no supreme fiction. The writing does end at a moment when Faulkner has recently surveyed his entire past output and defined the place at which the career has arrived. That definition, however, is not a breaking of the pencil which completes the task or abandons it, but a passing of the baton to the future, to the stranger a hundred years hence.

7

The Character of the Author

The knowledge won by Gavin Stevens at the end of the Snopes trilogy applies with equal pertinence to the world he inhabits and to Faulkner's career as a creator of such fictional worlds. The fate of design is to be transformed. In the happiest outcome, when it manifests a disciplined responsiveness to inherited designs and a responsibility for their future, the fate of design is to trace a coherent career. The successive moments will then form an array of designs that are both intimately related to one another and yet relatively autonomous, like the succession of cultural forms in Yoknapatawpha's fictional history or the sequence of texts in Faulkner's writing career. One begins always within a world whose designs are already given, But to make a career which can perpetuate the world's vitality and motion requires that the designs be ceaselessly and conscientiously transformed. Simply adopting a previous design or repeating it is to be made over in its image and so to become sterile. Such is the fate of Flem Snopes. The opposite and equally unhappy course stems from Thomas Sutpen's vain attempt to break with the past and create an original design. Aesthetically speaking, Flem Snopes is the cleverest copyist in the Academy, and Thomas Sutpen the iconoclast who hearkens only to his own genius. In contrast to such caricatures of the neoclassical and the romantic artist, Faulkner requires of himself a disciplined struggle with the past in order to make possible a future.

The parallels among the careers of a character, a society, and a writer can be taken still further. In representing any such career, the privileged genre is narrative. For it is the peculiar, though not exclusive power of narrative to depict both the individual constellations of experience which are the episodes or moments in a career and the succession from one moment to the next. Faulkner's mature narrative method expressly takes this as its task. "There's always a moment in experience—a thought—an incident—that's there. Then all I do is work up to that moment. I figure what must have happened before to lead people to that particular moment, and I work away from it, finding out how people act after that moment. That's how all my books and stories come" (*LG* 220). Faulkner's writing begins with a poetics of the transcendent moment of arrested motion, and he never loses his fascination with such times, when flux seems to stand frozen and complete. But as the writing then develops over the next thirty years, his books continually emphasize the imbrication of such moments in their antecedents and consequences. The moments within any given tale and those of the career itself exist both in their distinct individuality and as episodes in a larger course, the latter perspective revealing on the one hand how each moment grows out of, builds upon, and transforms its predecessors and on the other how it confesses its own lack of finality and so makes way for successors.

Narrative is also a privileged genre for a critical study of the writer's career. The usual difficulties of design and point of view necessarily apply. Like any story, this tale of Faulkner's career is constructed, even fictive, though I would not have narrated it as I have without believing that the materials lend themselves to this particular construction. I emphasize this not in order to rehearse simple truisms about the similarity between creative and critical discourse or to make a hopeless bid for aesthetic glory, but to identify Faulkner's relation to his career. He is here the main character in the story of the career.

Our final question, then, concerns the protagonist of the tale. Who or what is the figure of William Faulkner which serves as the hero of the story? Or rather, since the proper name also designates the historical personage who is doubtless only obscurely visible in this work, what is there about the writing which is characteristically Faulknerian and which limns for us a portrait of the artist? The question is one to conclude with because it summons the author, the one who is produced by the work, rather than the writing subject whose function is largely exhausted in producing it. Describing the author as a kind of character within a narrative necessarily places him within a controversy that has gone on for a long time and doubtless admits of no universally definitive resolution. Is a character the totality of his represented actions, or is he something more than that, an essence manifested in action and practice but not wholly comprised by them? My polemic intention is to argue that with Faulkner the former is more truly the case.

My use of "author" is more than a little semantically perverse, of course, for the term familiarly designates the independent originator of some expression. But the more consequential meaning of the word is the person who rightfully possesses an expression. Such rights need not be related to an a priori power or to temporal precedence. In the *Leviathan,* for example, Hobbes defines an author as the owner of the words and actions which represent him. Such ownership is his "authority," his "right of doing any act," and Hobbes explicitly compares it to the possession of property.[1] Hobbes implies that valid authority normally precedes its application,

1. Thomas Hobbes, *Leviathan, Parts I and II,* Herbert W. Schneider, ed. (Indianapolis 1958), 133.

but the implication is by no means necessary in his work or in Faulkner's. The *Leviathan* itself is expressly meant as an attack on the necessary authority of what is older and more established—the philosphy of the Greeks and the scholastics. More important, half a dozen passages in Faulkner's work tell us that true ownership rarely precedes its exercise. We need only recall *Absalom, Absalom!* to remember how much the possessor is a creature of his possessions.

Hobbes's concern is politics. So ultimately is Michel Foucault's in a brilliant article that more sharply defines what is at stake in the literary concept of the author.[2] Foucault points out that authorship is the historically conditioned invention of the culture which receives and transmits someone's writings. As such, it use varies with time and with the type of writings to which it is applied. Scientific works, for which the name of an author such as Galen or Aristotle was once essential, now belong to the collective and effectively anonymous authority of the science itself. What Euclid once authored is now ascribed to geometry. Literary works, for which anonymity was once more common and quite unremarkable, are now strictly attributed to a creative source who exists outside them and previous to them.

Foucault's most acutely polemic argument against this idea of the literary author is that it is ideological, by which he means precisely and pejoratively that it serves a social function the opposite of the one claimed for it. We think of the author as a benevolent font of meaning, but we secretly use him to control the proliferation of meaning in his texts. Meaning is limited to what is congruent with an assumption of authorial unity, consistency, and constancy. That assumption is the fundamental idea of the author for us.

2. Michel Foucault, "Qu'est-ce qu'un auteur?" *Bulletin de la société française de philosophie*, 63 (July–September 1969), 75–95; translated by Donald F. Bouchard in Foucault, *Language, Counter-Memory, Practice: Selected Essays and Interviews* (Ithaca, N.Y. 1977).

Examples of how this idea works are not difficult to come by. Consider the *auteur* theory of cinema as debated in France and more recently in the United States. Both advocates and critics of the theory agree that the debate turns on whether genuine singularity may be discerned in a particular director's films. Within the more immediate domain of literature, the use of the author as a limiting concept can readily be observed in textual scholarship and in the attribution of disputed works. One certifies authorship by showing the disputed work's similarity to undisputed works by the same person. Much the same idea applies in our understanding of an author whose works are not in question. The character of such an author is likely to be reconceived as our interpretation of his works changes, but at each point he is thought to be a principle of unity or at most an origin for the primary antinomy in his works.

According to such an idea, Faulkner's texts would be effectively limited to what is Faulknerian in them, the remainder being simply ignored or ascribed to confusion, posturing, or a falling away from his essential genius. In the 1930s, when Faulkner was widely considered a naturalist, the poetic and rhetorical elements in his writings had to be considered obfuscations or lapses. Later, when he became known for his complicated sentences, the relative directness of *As I Lay Dying* and much of *The Sound and the Fury* and *Light in August,* three of his most popular novels, seems to have been largely overlooked. Neither of these simplifications would be given much credence now, but even the ablest critical descriptions of the essentially Faulknerian make the same assumptions of unity.

Foucault's critique seems to me unassailable as long as the author is understood to be a static, well-nigh marmoreal figure whose signature on the title page or whose authentication by a textual scholar guards the writing from straying beyond bounds. Understanding Faulkner as such a unitary author would make him the name of a uniformity which limits his writings to what they all have in common. But if one were truly to consider all his writings, one would inevitably find their continuity to lie in the lowest common denominators of style, theme, and method. There are such constants in the writings, ranging from trivialities—the books were all written in English—to more interesting ones—the potency of the arrested motion concept. But Faulkner the author, the protagonist in this or any other narrative of his career, is not an unchanging essence who exists before his works and outside of them. Like any of his characters, he is the "sum of his past," a past that constantly changes throughout his life as a writer (*FU* 84). We have seen in tracing the career how this past affects his writings. It both impels him to go beyond what he has done and conditions the directions in which he will move. Both consequences are important to a more accurate understanding of his authorship.

Faulkner's authority is for him first an enabling claim or an arrogation, like those made by Thomas Sutpen in setting out to create his dynasty. Faulkner deems himself an author in order to be able to become one in fact. But for us and ultimately for Faulkner in the career as well, his authority is largely established and maintained by his continuing responsibility for writings so enabled and by his responses to them. The authority is in fact most persuasively established by the challenges that subsequent texts make to the provisional assumptions and premises of earlier ones. Faulkner's authorship likewise results from his having continually altered old methods, styles, themes, and purposes. It derives, in effect, from the *lack* of uniformity in a career which always strays beyond previous bounds and disrupts established continuities. Without that straying, so we have seen it strongly implied, the writing would not have been possible at all. Certainly it would have been very different and indeed very unFaulknerian. Faulkner the author is thus not a static essence but a procession of transformations. The figure of his authorship is the disciplined mobility inscribed within the transformations of his career. Both author and authority are thus largely retroactive creations of the career's changing trajectory. Both are products of the self-established discipline to which the writer adheres in making his writing a coherent career.

Index

Absalom, Absalom!, 24, 28, 34, 121, 123–156, 160–161, 184–185, 198; as critique of *As I Lay Dying*, 28, 133–135; design as act in, 126–127, 131–133; design as intention in, 126–127, 136–139, 141–145, 151; design as pattern in, 126–127, 130–131; enabling principles of, 123–141; failure of design in, 127–136; inheritance and ownership in, 135–136, 198

Adams, Richard, 33, 99

"Admonishes His Heart," 51

"Adolescence," 42, 48, 51

"April," 46

Armstids, the, 118, 169, 174, 179–180

Arrested motion, 33–35, 42, 45–46, 62, 68–70, 73–75, 79, 101–103, 123–126, 149, 154–159, 189–190, 196, 200; as artistic paradigm, 33–35, 78–80, 123–125, 149, 159, 193; as theme, 33, 42, 70, 101–103

Artistic principles, Faulkner's, 33–39, 60–61, 75, 78–80, 91–93, 134–135, 193–195; definitions of art and artistic purpose, 33, 61–68, 91–93, 97, 149; impersonality, 96, 104, 125–128, 141; obligations and responsibilities of the artist, 35–39, 56–57, 147, 157–160; representational and referential, 96–100, 112–113, 125–128; visionary, 33, 42–45, 53–57, 61–63, 67–69, 75–78

Ashby, W. Ross, 31

As I Lay Dying, 27–29, 94–123, 128–141, 149, 153–154, 158, 182, 199; enabling principles of, 94–106, 134; horizontal and vertical imagery in, 96–98, 101–117; language and consciousness in, 106–115, 119; motion as theme in, 94–122; narrative technique of, 94–101; relation of characters to past and present in, 108–121

"Aubade," 58

Author, defined, 18–20; Faulkner's character as, 37–40, 97, 195–201

Authority, 19, 39–40, 197–201

Balzac, Honoré de, 29–30, 63, 68

"Barn Burning," 176

Bateson, Gregory, 31

Beardsley, Aubrey, 72

"Bear Hunt, A," 175

Beauchamp, Lucas, 156, 159

Beauchamp, Molly, 159, 187

Benbow, Horace, 79, 100, 125

Bible, 158

Blotner, Joseph, 16, 68, 164

Bon, Charles, 129, 137, 144–145, 148, 152

Bookwright, 168, 180

Bradford, M. E., 106

Brod, Max 19

Brooks, Cleanth, 20, 53–54, 143

Brothers Karamazov, 97

Browning, Robert, 95–96

Bunch, Byron, 101, 124

Bundren, Addie, 102–103, 106–122, 132, 154; as exponent of horizontal consciousness, 106–115

Bundren, Anse, 101–102, 107–111, 116

Bundren, Cash, 102–103, 107–108, 110, 118–122, 124, 128, 134, 149, 154

Bundren, Darl, 100, 102, 105, 110–120, 126, 134; as exponent of vertical consciousness, 110–115; madness of, 105, 114–115; narrative powers of, 105, 110

Bundren, Dewey Dell, 102–103, 105, 108, 111, 113, 116, 119–120

Bundren, Jewel, 102, 111, 114, 116, 120

Bundren, Vardaman, 102–103, 108, 110, 116–117

Burden, Joanna, 100

"By the People," 181

"Carcassonne," 57

Career, literary, 13–44, 62–67, 96–98, 135, 141–143, 151, 161–166, 195–201; and authority, 19, 39–40, 200–201; and enabling principles, 26–28, 33–34, 37; Faulkner's ideas about, 35–39; general concept of, 14–19, 23, 28–29, 30–33; and literary materials, 24–25, 35, 62–65, 134–136, 138, 141–143, 146, 151; and literary tradition, 21, 23–25, 29, 43–44, 56, 58, 61, 96–98, 145, 151, 166, 193–194; as system and discipline, 14–40; as theme, 14, 152, 164, 183–192; threats to coherence of, 37–39, 152

"Cathedral in the Rain," 46

Christmas, Joe, 38, 98, 100–101, 124, 186

Clytie (daughter of Thomas Sutpen), 144

Coldfield, Rosa, 127, 129–131, 137–138, 145–151, 154

Collected Stories of William Faulkner, 57, 176

Comédie Humaine, 29

"Compson Appendix," 86, 88

Compson, Benjy, 77, 80–88, 92, 124, 154

Compson, Caddy, 75–81, 84–87, 92, 100, 148

Compson, General, 127, 143

Compson, Jason, 76, 81, 85–90, 132, 158

Compson, Mr., 86–87, 127–137

Compson, Quentin, 37–39, 45, 52, 76–92, 100, 125–156, 185; in *Absalom, Absalom!*, 125–145; as designer, 125, 136–152; and the poetry, 45–61; in *The Sound and the Fury*, 77–93

Conrad, Joseph, 25, 63

Cowley, Malcom, 62, 159

Critical theory, 19–27, 196–197

Cummings, E. E., 53

Cybernetics, 30–33

Day, Douglas, 63

Debussy, Claude, 44

Dedalus, Stephen, 96

Design. *See* Forms and fiction *and Absalom, Absalom!*

De Spain, Mayor, 162–163, 182

Dilsey, 89–92, 176

Don Quixote, 118

"Doomsday Book," 30

Dostoevski, Feodor, 63, 97

Drake, Temple, 100

"Drowning," 45

Ducdame, 64

Early Prose and Poetry. See William Faulkner; Early Prose and Poetry

Edmonds, McCaslin ("Cass"), 21

Elegy. *See* Genre

Eliot, T. S., 43–44, 53, 96, 98; "Tradition and the Individual Talent," 96; *The Waste Land*, 98

"Elmer," 64

Emerson, Ralph Waldo, 186

Enabling principles, 26–37, 94–95; of *Absalom, Absalom!*, 123–141; of *As I Lay Dying*, 94–106, 134; and career, 27–28, 33–34, 37, 164; defined, 26–27, 94; of the early fiction, 70–75; of the poetry, 41–60; of the Snopes trilogy, 164–166; of *The Sound and the Fury*, 75–80, 92–93

Essays, Speeches, and Public Letters of William Faulkner, 16, 37, 64

"Eunice," 54

Fable, A, 17, 125–126, 156, 160–161, 192

Failure, Faulkner's understanding of, 59–60

Fairchild, Dawson, 68, 74–75, 78–79
"Father Abraham," 63
Faulkner in the University, 36–38, 56, 59, 64, 68, 76, 102, 114, 129, 131, 134, 147, 160, 193, 200
"Faun, The," 50
Finn, Huckleberry, 175, 177
"Fire and the Hearth, The," 159
Flags in the Dust. See Sartoris
Flaubert, Gustave, 25, 63, 68, 158
"Flowers That Died, The," 47
"Fool About a Horse," 167
Forms and fiction, 25, 29, 41, 61, 69, 96–98, 106–115, 123–152, 157; 160–195; and cultural institutions, 139, 146, 152, 157, 160–181, 195; failure of, 130–152; literary, 25, 29, 41, 61, 69, 96–98, 146–148, 160, 163, 168, 180–181, 185–194; as psychological defenses, 124–137
Foucault, Michel, 23, 198–200
Franklin, R. W., 105
Frye, Northrop, 20

Genius, writer's relation to, 24, 146, 151–152
Genius loci, writer's relation to, 24, 146, 151–152
Genre, 41–43, 57–64, 72–73, 161–195; elegy as meta-fiction, 161–194; Faulkner's use of traditional, 63, 166, 190–195; poetry vs. prose, 41–43, 57–64, 72–73
Girard, René, 183
Go Down, Moses, 21, 139, 151, 158–161, 187, 192, 194
Gold, Joseph, 173
Goodyhay, Brother, 188
Green Bough, A, 45–58, 69–70, 73
Grimm, Eustace, 173
Grimm, Percy, 98
Grove, Lena, 98, 101, 124
Guetti, James, 132–134

Hamlet, The, 124, 153, 159–185, 191–192; despair in, 178–181; humor in, 168–178; male myth in, 168–178. *See also* Snopes trilogy
Hardy, Thomas, 51, 98
Harris, George Washington, 175

Hartman, Geoffrey, 24–25, 146, 151–152
Head, Herbert, 86
Hegel, Georg Wilhelm Friedrich, 32
"Helen and the Centaur," 51, 58
Hemingway, Ernest, 36, 38
Heraclitus, 101
Hergesheimer, Joseph, 64, 74–75
Hightower, Wayne, 37, 98
Hipps, Buck, 173–174
Hobbes, Thomas, 197–198
Housman, A. E., 45, 50, 58; *A Shropshire Lad,* 58
Houston, Jack, 168, 170, 174, 187, 191
Howard, Alan, 177
Hulme, T. E., 96
Husserl, Edmund, 137
Huxley, Aldous, 74
"Hymn," 51–52, 58

Irwin, John, 136
"I Will Not Weep for Youth," 47

James, Henry, 63
Jesus Christ, 84, 90–92, 115
Jones, Januarius, 72
Joyce, James, 36, 96–97

Kafka, Franz, 19
Keats, John, 42, 57, 70–71, 99–100, 158, 184; "Ode on a Grecian Urn," 70
Kohl, Linda Snopes, *See* Snopes, Linda

Labove, 168–171, 176
Language, 23, 71–75, 106–113, 121–126, 135–136, 151, 157–159
"L'Apres-Midi d'un Faune," 44, 55
Leviathan, 197–198
Levine, 125
Lévi-Strauss, Claude, 130, 139
Light in August, 37, 84, 98, 100, 104, 124, 126, 160, 182, 199
Linda Condon, 73–74
Lion in the Garden, 33, 35–36, 42, 59–60, 97, 115, 118, 135, 142, 149, 176, 196
Littlejohn, Mrs., 168, 177
'Lizards in Jamshyd's Courtyard," 175
Lukács, Georg, 65–68, 73
Luster, 86
Luvingood, Sut, 175

McCannon, Shreve (called Shreve MacKenzie in *The Sound and the Fury*), 127–135, 144
McCarron, Hoake, 171
McCaslin, Carothers, 21
McCaslin, Ike, 21, 38, 151, 155–156
McEacherns, the, 186
Mackay, Donald M., 31
Mahon, Donald, 72–73
Mallarmé, Stéphane, 36, 43–44
Mallison, Charles, 156, 159, 163, 189
Mannigoe, Nancy, 156, 187
Mansion, The, 38–39, 162–167, 174–193. *See also* Snopes trilogy
Marble Faun, The, 46–51, 96
Marx, Karl, 174
Mauss, Marcel, 167
Meredith, George, 74
Meriwether, James B., 15, 26, 42–43, 63–65, 80, 105–106, 141
Millgate, Michael, 98, 161, 164
Milton, John, 190
Modernism, 43–46, 66, 96–97, 158
Mosquitoes, 25, 63, 68–69, 74–78
"Mule in the Yard," 181

Narrative, 33, 41–58, 61–106, 133–136, 160–201; Faulkner's narrative methods, 33, 61–93, 160–165, 195–201; narration and description, 65–67; the novel as genre, 41–58, 61–65, 70, 196–201; realistic tradition of the novel, 61, 66, 93, 98, 158
"New Orleans," 71, 79
New Orleans Sketches. See William Faulkner: New Orleans Sketches
Nobel Prize speech, 64
Novel. *See* Narrative

Orpheus, 56

Pan, 47–51
Passion story, 160
Pastoral, 41–61, 76, 166–167, 190–194; as poetic realm, 46, 53–55, 91; in Snopes trilogy, 166–167
Pate, Lucy, 170
Peabody, Doc, 118
Peacock, Thomas Love, 74
Petrie, Peter, 159

Phases of Faulkner's career, 34; concern with designing, 123–152; defined, 94–95; elegiac, 153–194; referential, 94–122; visionary, 41–60
Poe, Edgar Allan, 130
Poetry, Faulkner's, 41–63, 69–72, 76–85, 92; aesthetic principles of, 44–45, 63; failure of, 41, 63. *See also entries for individual poems*
Poirier, Richard, 53–54
Popeye, 100
Pouillon, Jean, 117
Pound, Ezra, 44, 96
Powers, Margaret, 72
Powys, John Cowper, 64
Proust, Marcel, 29
Pylon, 38, 116, 147

Ranke, Leopold von, 32
Ratliff, V. K., 159, 163, 167–181, 185–192; challenge to values of, 179–184; and frontier humor, 168–180; as spokesman for male myth, 167–175
Reader, the, 39, 41, 43–44, 66, 78, 85, 92, 105, 121–123, 129, 154, 183, 200
Reba, Miss, 188
Reed, Joseph, 65
Reivers, The, 161, 194
Requiem for a Nun, 161, 187, 192
Rittenmeyer, Charlotte, 156–158
Robyn, Patricia, 48

Said, Edward, 15
Sanctuary, 94, 100, 125, 192
Sartoris, 63, 79, 175, 192
Sartoris, Bayard, 38, 151, 156
Sartoris/Flags in the Dust. See Sartoris
Sartoris, John, 156
Sartre, Jean-Paul, 32
Saunders, Cecily, 48
Saussure, Ferdinand de, 157
Scribner's Magazine, 65
Selected Letters of William Faulkner, 27, 129, 160
Shakespeare, William, 30, 57
Shegog, Reverend, 90
Shelley, Percy Bysshe, 95, 190
"Shingles for the Lord," 192
Simon, John K., 103
Slatoff, Walter, 59

Snopes, Ab, 166–169, 174–176
Snopes, Eula Varner. *See* Varner, Eula
Snopes, Flem, 38, 146, 155, 158–164,
   172–189, 199; career of, 163–164; use
   of forms and rituals, 155, 172–181
Snopes, Ike, 124, 154, 169, 176–179,
   191
Snopes, I. O., 178
Snopes, Linda, 39, 159, 182–184, 188
Snopes, Lump, 173
Snopes, Mink, 38, 162, 167–178, 185–
   193; apotheosis of, 192–193; trusting
   and depending, 185–191
Snopes, Montgomery Ward, 162, 182–
   183
Snopes, St. Elmo, 179
Snopes trilogy, 153–195; composition
   of, 153, 161–166; 180–181; as elegy,
   160–194; enabling principles of,
   165–166; failure in, 178–194; forms
   of exchange in, 185–186; relation of
   men and women in, 168–182; rituals, forms, and institutions, 161–
   194; values in, 157, 160–194
Soldiers' Pay, 29, 63, 71–79
Sound and the Fury, The, 52, 59–95, 99–
   104, 132, 153–154, 160–166, 192,
   199; displacement of timeless ideal in,
   61–93; narrative methods of, 61–93;
   relation to the poetry, 63–70
Spilka, Mark, 21, 85
"Spotted Horses," 175
Stamper, Pat, 167
Stevens, Gavin, 98, 156–163, 178–195
Stevens, Wallace, 39, 96
Subjectivity, 18, 80, 88–89, 103, 109–
   112, 114–117, 123–125, 136–138,
   153–155
Sutpen, Henry, 144
Sutpen, Judith, 148
Sutpen, Thomas, 38, 126–154, 158,
   161, 185, 195, 200; as designer, 126–
   145, 161; relation to materiality,
   137–142, 185
Swinburne, Algernon, 44, 77–78

Tennyson, Alfred, 190
Themes in Faulkner's work: the absolute and the timeless, transcendent
   ideal, 45–60, 71, 76–80, 82–93, 114;

arrested motion, 33–35, 45–46, 62,
   68–70, 73–75, 79, 101–103, 123,
   149, 155–159, 189–190, 196–200;
   desire, 45–60, 71, 76, 86, 123–126;
   fate of designs and fictions, 151,
   155–158, 161–194; life as motion,
   36–37, 99–122, 184, 189–190, 193;
   selfhood and consciousness, 42, 52,
   71, 79, 81–82, 89–90, 102–103, 105,
   109–117, 123, 136–138, 154–155;
   time and change, 36–37, 42, 47–48,
   70, 72–73, 75, 78, 80–82, 84, 88, 90,
   101, 103–109, 148, 190; values and
   morality, 118, 156–158, 160–194
Town, The, 161–162, 164, 178, 181–
   185. *See also* Snopes trilogy
Tull, Cora, 118
Tull, Vernon, 109, 118, 170
Twain, Mark, 158, 175

"Uncle Willy," 192
Unvanquished, The, 151, 155

Varner, Eula, 163, 169, 171–172, 176–
   177, 182
Varner, Jody, 173, 178
Varner, Will, 166–177
Verlaine, Paul, 44
Vickery, Olga, 20, 129

Wall, Carey, 77
Wilbourne, Harry, 151, 156–158
Wilden, Anthony, 31, 139
Wild Palms, The, 151, 155, 158, 164,
   182
*William Faulkner: Early Prose and Poet-
   ry,* 50, 55, 57–58, 64, 73–74, 96,
   135–136
William Faulkner: New Orleans Sketches,
   69
Williams, William Carlos, 96, 134
Wiseman, Eva, 69
Wiseman, Julius, 75
Writer, 18–23

Yeats, William Butler, 32, 44, 96
Yoknapatawpha County, 29–30, 37,
   62, 146, 164, 167, 183, 195

Zeno, 101

FAULKNER'S CAREER

Designed by R. E. Rosenbaum. Composed by Huron Valley Graphics in 11 point VIP Bembo, 2 points leaded, with display lines in VIP Bembo. Printed offset by Thomson/Shore, Inc. on Warren's No. 66 Antique Offset, 50 pound basis. Bound by John H. Dekker and Sons in Holliston book cloth, with stamping in All Purpose foil.

Library of Congress Cataloging in Publication Data

(For library cataloging purposes only)
Stonum, Gary Lee.
    Faulkner's career.

    Includes index.
    1. Faulkner, William, 1897–1962—Criticism and
interpretation. I. Title.
PS3511.A86Z9728   813′. 5′2   78-23503
ISBN 0-8014-1196-3